# Loaves and Hyacinths:

 *Tea Rooms in London and East Anglia*

# Loaves and Hyacinths:
## Tea Rooms in London and East Anglia

By

Gladys S. Lewis, *Author*

and

Norma K. Brown, *Artist*

GREYSTONE PRESS
Edmond, Oklahoma
1999

Library of Congress Cataloging-in-Publication Data

Lewis, Gladys S. and Norma K. Brown
Loaves and Hyacinths: Tea rooms in London and East Anglia

Selected tea rooms in London and East Anglia for a
focus on history, literature, and art through the British
tea customs.

Library of Congress Catalog Number
99-94360

ISBN: 0-9669682-0-4 Hardback: alk. paper

Printed by EBSCO Graphics
1223 Linwood Boulevard
Oklahoma City, Oklahoma 73106

GREYSTONE PRESS
Edmond, Oklahoma
1999

*An English Tea Room*

*Hyacinths for the Soul*

# Loaves and Hyacinths
## ⊷ *Precedents* ⊶

If of thy mortal goods thou art bereft,
And from thy slender store
   Two loaves alone to thee are left,
Sell one, and with the dole
   Buy hyacinths to feed thy soul.

> Attributed to the Gulistan of Moslih Eddin Saadi (1184-1291)
> Persian poet and Muslim Sheik
> *Best Loved Poems of the American People* (1936)

If thou of fortune be bereft
And in thy store there be but left
Two loaves, sell one and with the dole
Buy hyacinths to feed thy soul.

> From "Not By Bread Alone," by James Terry White (1845-1920)
> Adaptation by James Terry White
> *Century Magazine* (August 1907)

**If you have money for two loaves, buy one,
and hyacinths for the soul.**

> Paraphrase by Gladys S. Lewis
> *Loaves and Hyacinths* (1999)

# Table of Contents

## ⤙⟶ *Tea Rooms* ⟵⤚

# Paintings

*Front pages:* An English Tea Room
Hyacinths for the Soul

# Foreword

The idea for this book came first to the artist, dubbed Sergeant-Major by the writer, who then labeled herself Archivist-Navigator because she kept records and read maps in the book's research process. Norma Brown, the Sergeant-Major, lived all her life with a dream to paint in England. With her first pilgrimage there from Oklahoma, she became an anglophile, particularly enchanted by English tea rooms. She searched book stores to learn more about them. No specific information was in print in England or America. Books about tea, yes; but, she found nothing which treated the tea room, that quintessential social microcosm which reflects so much of greater Britain. Intrigued, she determined to write a book about them from an artist's perspective. With more deliberation, she decided the subject was broader than her first conclusions, and that it had merit as a book with wider appeal than one restricted to an art audience. She contacted a writer friend with her idea. I, Gladys Lewis, the Navigator-Archivist, also a lover of all things British, with earliest reading memories of Beowulf and Grendel and the King Arthur legends which have since grown to encompass a Ph.D. in literature, became ink for Brown's paint.

Our research trip to East Anglia overwhelmed with joy and discovery, jeopardy and dilemma. We pulsed to experiences of touching our roots, visiting the geography of our ancestral origins, and viewing places which had triggered aesthetic expression from other writers and painters. We stalled at getting lost, misunderstanding British English, and puzzling over people not knowing where a place was if it were not located next door. After a particularly trying morning, attempting to function as Navigator-Archivist in

Aldeburgh, I asked the Sergeant-Major, "Are these the people who circumnavigated the globe and founded an empire? Or, are these the ones who stayed home?"

Yet the allure that the British hold, by being a people who can remain private and individual while living in a scale model world set on the frontier of Apocalypse, kept pulling us, making us circumnavigate road-honeycombed shires. We were on a quest as surely as Sir Gawain hunted the Green Knight, Spenser's Red Cross Knight strove to serve Gloriana, Queen Elizabeth's fleet searched for the Spanish Armada, or the Raj ruled India for Victoria. All the tea rooms of East Anglia lay before us, and we intended to visit as many as possible in our broadened vision of England as viewed through her tea rooms. We believe the tea room and custom of taking tea uniquely transmit British character. In a global technocracy, England is its own Camelot. Competitors for the prizes we all seek, the English stop each busy day to take tea, allow soul and body communal (and communion) time, and relax about life. When American bombers flew from East Anglian bases to Libya and Chernobyl misted radioactivity across Europe, people read and discussed events at tea time. We were with them. The happenings seemed less threatening over a cup of Ceylon's best with a clotted-cream-covered scone.

How could we shape a book about the quintessence of tea rooms to capture some of those qualities that have made England the seedbed for the world's dominant cultural force in government, history, language, and literature? We pondered the thought as a routine conversation topic. The second flame was struck by the Navigator-Archivist.

We had left our set tea at the Savoy's Thames Foyer to go out by Victoria Embankment on the Thames. Trailing our hands all the way down a polished brass bannister two flights, we saw a maid cleaning the last two carpeted steps with a feather duster. Walking through the park, we stood hushed by a sunken bed of gorgeous pink, white, and purple hyacinths across from Robert Burns's brooding statue. Sergeant-Major talked of a poem about hyacinths by James Terry White, "Not By Bread Alone," an adaptation of a Persian motif, with this basic theme: "If you have two loaves, sell one, and buy hyacinths for the soul."

Later, overlooking a garden from the dining room of the Marlborough Hotel in Ipswich, I, Navigator-Archivist, proposed a variation on our paraphrase about loaves and hyacinths as a unifying symbol for words, paint, and subject: a metaphorical treatment that would consider the areas we visited, and tea rooms as the hyacinths. Bread, the symbol of life, is like Britain to us: the basic nutrient that gives us a cultural base as Americans. We are ardent nationalists, not ex-patriots. But we taste the grain of our beginnings as a deep comforting strength within us and find joy in the nourishment. The loaves, as we found them, gave strength to our search. The hyacinths, the tea rooms, growing among them, energized our spirits.

In artistic agreement, with ink and color, we propose selected tea shops as hyacinths among the loaves we found in London and East Anglia. This is not a travel book, though we criss-crossed the hamlets, villages, and towns of East Anglia. Neither is it a food critic's guide, though we ate in more than fifty tea rooms. This book is our ink and color interpretation of a significant journey through our historical, artistic, and spiritual loaves that was reinforced by the supportive, fragrant hyacinths we encountered. Like the early explorers who brought home tea while expanding their kingdom, we searched for an empire within ourselves where we, too, can be both private and individual in a macrocosm of impersonality. Hunting for tea rooms in a technocracy seems to symbolize the pilgrimage.

# Dedication

*To Lavonn Brown and Wilbur Lewis,*
*rocks both, who hold loosely the long tethers of freedom*
*connected to shoppers for loaves and seekers*
*of hyacinths.*

# Introduction

## ⟶⟹ *Tea Rooms* ⟸⟵

Tea rooms are a development of the last hundred years. In England, they have become a logical extension of the British economic and colonial involvement with the tea producing regions of the world. Tea's ancient history and ritual enactments produced a uniquely compatible vehicle for cultural interchange in the British environment. Showcasing the special character of performance choreographed between place, food, and communication, the tea room provides a stage for subtle indigenous drama. Volumes exist which take as subject coffeehouses, but little is recorded of tea rooms. The original ones were limited in appeal to women. They provided a place for afternoon tea and talk. Men remarked that more scandal originated in them than "hovered over the court of Good Queen Bess." The tea room became the women's lodge, or the men's coffeehouse counterpart.

The tea room made its debut when restaurants had indifferent interiors and carelessly prepared food which was unattractively served. In contrast, tea rooms were small, snug, and homey places. With the evolution of more substantial menus and the endurance of tea time, they have become centers for men as well as for women. Tea rooms are not exclusively British, being found throughout the world as they are. But those encountered in England have a distinctive atmosphere. The principles of harmony, respect, purity of a custom, and tranquility, as practiced in Oriental tea ceremonies, are not expressed in the same manner in the English tea room, but the qualities are present. The following chapters of this book will treat the geography, history, social and literary environment, appurtenances, and fare of selected tea rooms in London and East Anglia.

*Tea at the Savoy — London*

# I.

# London Loaves and Hyacinths
### ⊸⇒ *Thames Foyer in the Savoy Hotel* ⇐⊷

Taking tea anywhere, in the British manner, is a lovely experience. Doing so in one of London's premier hotels rises to an event. The pinnacle of civilized elegance must be "set tea" in the Thames Foyer of the Savoy. Creme tea, served from 3:30 to 5:30 in the afternoon, blooms as an exquisite hyacinth set among the loaves of sustenance discovered on every corner of historic London.

The Thames Foyer's decor recreates a garden setting. Mauve, pink, and green in the carpet and furniture patterns structure the outdoor theme. In the room's middle, a white gazebo houses the hotel's famous white baby grand piano and accentuates the mood. Corinthian columns circle the area. Murals, appearing as arched windows with painted pastoral scenes beyond, expand the foyer to a country environment. *Art nouveau* mirrors from the 1911 coronation festivities of King George V reach the ceiling and, with the restaurant stretching into the background, extend the size of the foyer.

The foyer, the hyacinth, introduces the loaf, the Savoy, but the two overlap. Tasting one means savoring the other. To partake of the loaf that is the Savoy is to eat the bread of our cultural and political past. Though created in 1980, in its current decor and name, the Thames Foyer, as part of the Savoy Hotel, stands on property that has had significance since 1246 when King Henry III gave a tract of land to Queen Eleanor's uncle, Count Peter of Savoy. Located between London and Westminster, Savoy Hill had an annual rent of three barbed arrows. Peter built a magnificent palace and played matchmaker between English peers and the beautiful French noblewomen whom he hosted. Resentment of his foreign influence eventuated in his return to the Continent. His property went to John of Gaunt, Duke of Lancaster, uncle of Richard II, and the real ruler behind the boy king's throne. John lived in the Savoy palace twenty years. From his largesse came a grant for ten pounds a year for the poet Geoffrey Chaucer, a sum paid at the Manor of Savoy. Though unsubstantiated, tradition has *The Canterbury Tales* planned, and perhaps written, within the old palace. However, from John's greed came such heavy taxes that a rebellion, led by Wat Tyler, ignited in 1381 and resulted in destruction of the palace. Sacked and burned, it lay in ruins more than a century.

In 1399, John's son became Henry VI, the first king of the House of Lancaster, and the Duchy of Lancaster went to the Crown, with the old Savoy estate becoming the location for Duchy head-quarters and being called the Liberty of the Manor of Savoy. Henry VII, first Tudor king, rebuilt the decayed palace for use as a charity hospital. Oliver Cromwell ordered a Confession of Faith written at Savoy in 1658, and Charles II decreed an ecclesiastical meeting on the site in 1660 which produced the Revised Prayer Book. In 1773, the Duchy of Lancaster took over maintenance responsibility and started repairs on the chapel that had survived the estate's turbulent history. Long considered a chapel royal, it became one in fact in 1937. In the Coronation Honours List of George VI, it was pro-claimed King's Chapel, which made it a private chapel of the Sover-eign and free from ecclesiastical ties to the Archbishop of Canter-bury. Today, Queen Elizabeth II is Lady of the Manor; the Savoy Chapel is a royal chapel and the home of the Royal Victorian Order; and the Duchy of Lancaster, bequest of John of Gaunt, headquarters in the Liberty of the Savoy. During World War II, the Chapel was a bright spot, with war-time romances culminating in marriages, and happy couples making the brief walk to their reception in a confetti storm created by anyone in the hotel.

By the 1880s, the old Savoy Manor was unused land. An enterprising concert agent, Richard D'Oyly Carte, in partnership with the lyricist-composer team, Gilbert and Sullivan, bought the freehold on part of the manor land to build a performance center and launched The Savoy Theatre in 1881. Success followed success for the partners. Always the innovative entrepreneur, D'Oyly Carte turned his thoughts to possibilities for a luxury hotel between the theater and the Embankment. In 1889, after a five-year building period, the Savoy Hotel opened with an impressive list of architectural triumphs: lifts; soundproofing; shaded electric lights provided by the hotel's own power plant; warmed corridors; speaking-tubes for room service; and, most shocking, seventy bathrooms instead of the communal system of contemporary hotels. With a crusader's zeal, D'Orly Carte set about making the Savoy the standard bearer for setting, elegance, cuisine, service, and clientele. He was aided by several notable people: Lillie Langtry, an international beauty and a favorite of the Prince of Wales; Cesar Ritz, the first Hotel Manager, who eventually headed his own luxury establishment; and Escoffier, the *maitre-chef*, who created *peches Melba* and *toast Melba* for *prima donna*, Dame Nellie Melba, one of the hotel's early patrons. Subsequent staff and directors have maintained early standards of impeccable excellence.

The Savoy serves as a social registry for world figures. Sarah Bernhardt had a suite. Mark Twain was a guest. Marconi carried out his experiments in a room with additional sound-proofing where he lived. Extravagant banquets set the norm. On his birthday in 1905,

George A. Kessler, champagne millionaire and Wall Street financier, ordered the courtyard flooded and paid Caruso to sing from a gondolier. Winston Churchill and his political friend, F. E. Smith, founded The Other Club, which had regular dinners at the hotel, as an opportunity for public figures to be together privately. From 1927, because Churchill wished it, Kasper, a three-feet-tall wooden carved cat, attended every dinner of The Other Club. Kasper's creation was commissioned by the hotel. In the event of a party of thirteen, Kasper took the thirteenth chair with napkin around his neck, and was served course after course with the other diners.

After World War I, the Savoy was headquarters for Hoover's Relief Committees. Scott and Zelda Fitzgerald, John Barrymore, and the Russian Ballet crossed the foyer as arrivals. With the Jazz Age, it became a stage for international celebrities. Pavlova danced there — after her performances. Irving Berlin played his tunes. Marcus Loew and Sam Goldwyn used it as a base when making movie deals. Tetrazzini practiced her scales in counterpoint to Melba's, and cooked in Room 412 for her friends. On a given night, in separate dining rooms, the Savoy hosted Lord Balfour, Lord Beaverbrook, a group of Zionists, Charles Lindbergh, and King Faud with Bank of Egypt Governors. Obviously, the foyer was crowded.

London society, even Royalty, went to the ballroom for the years's progression of dance styles. Massachusetts-born Carroll Gibbons, with his white piano and orchestra, reigned for thirty years from the Turkey trot, through the Charleston, to the tango. The *dansant* (tea dance) originated at the Savoy, with tango teas showcasing the talents of stars like Valentino.

All the prominent people in entertainment, literary pursuits, and politics paraded through. With war threat across the channel, Anthony Eden briefed newsmen there as Joseph Kennedy looked on without speaking. Churchill was at the Savoy when the call came advising him he would take over No. 10 Downing Street. During the war, a river suite was reserved for his naps when he was too tired to return home. With World War II, the Savoy became the "Blitz Hotel." Fortified and blacked out, it was home to deposed sovereigns and presidents of nations routed by the Nazis; it served as base to newsmen like Ernie Pyle and Ed Murrow. Red Cross nurses tended people in it. The Gibbons musical broadcasts gave people outside the hotel a sense of stability. Noel Coward's songs at the white piano reassured those within the hotel.

The foyer has known all the hotel has witnessed. In its new garden landscape, it continues as a quiet oasis in the midst of a scurrying metropolis. Just waiting to be seated for tea is a retreat: resting on the huge circular sofa, feeling dwarfed by the enormous arrangements of cut flowers, looking at the gleaming tableware in the foyer. Set tea, the formal setting of a tea table with immaculate linen and table service, is done in the predominant pink and white, long a motif at the Savoy. Four huge chandeliers with white-painted metal roses entwine toward the ceiling. Waiters in black cutaways, still maintaining the wet-hair look, with attitudes as formal as their attire, stand at their posts. One seats guests, descending to the table between two reclining deer on pedestals flanking the stairs. Another lays a pink and white napkin with the gray embroidered *S* across laps. Another offers menus. Fare is the same for each guest. Menus simply communicate the offerings. Tea choice lies between Ceylon or the Savoy's blend of China tea. A succession of food arrives: sandwiches of smoked salmon, cucumber, tomato, and creamed eggs; scones with clotted-cream and strawberry (pronounced "straw-br'ee," with the *a* drawn out) jam; and pastries. Tea comes in the pink and white Wedgewood porcelain with the gray

S, hot water to freshen it in a matching pot, and cream and sugar in their respective containers of pink and white. Silver gleams with the patina of age, some of it so old that the engraved "Savoy" is barely seen.

A pause in such surroundings is an invitation to reverie. Eating from the Wedgewood recalls the Savoy's practice of ordering customized glass and porcelain from manufacturers. Fingering the perfectly laundered napkin reminds that all the hotel's Irish linen is woven to specification and, since 1921, cared for in the hotel laundry at Clapham. Throughout World War II, General Eisenhower sent his laundry to the Savoy in aluminum containers, even when he was in North Africa and France.

In the quiet of tea time, echoes come clearly: Tom Mix riding his horse, Tony, hooves padded, up the steps to the ballroom; George Gershwin playing "Rhapsody in Blue" for the first time in London; Sinclair Lewis's soft writing sounds as he started work on *Dodsworth*; Tallulah Bankhead calling, "Dah-ling," across the room; Maurice Chevalier crooning through his smiles; Alexander Korda of London Films speaking softly as he played Cupid to Laurence Olivier and Vivian Leigh; Andre Maurois scratching galley proofs as he corrected his biography of Dickens; Einstein clinking table silver as he dined quietly; Noel Coward and Gertrude Lawrence eating after a show; Gertrude Lawrence joking with Hemingway about breaking eggs on him; Hemingway announcing the arrival of "the Kraut," Marlene Dietrich; Clark Gable creating by his presence a female furor; President Truman speaking plainly on a State Visit; Mae West expressing surprise at RAF life jackets being named for her; Elizabeth Taylor filming there as a seventeen-year-old and honeymooning as an eighteen-year-old; Ed Murrow lying in the hotel's gutter with his microphone on the ground to capture air raid sounds for American audiences; more recent pilgrimages of the wealthy from

Commonwealth nations; and other celebrities such as Maria Callas, Stravinsky, Sister Kenny, the Shah of Iran, Chaplin. So many echoes . . . some reverberating around the Thames Foyer for nearly a century . . . others, more modern, like those of the voices that first planned the European Common Market.

Each year brings its yeast for the bread. The loaf remains fresh while retaining the old, familiar flavor. As does the hyacinth, The Thames Foyer continues to bloom. To have tea there is to acquire an aesthetic memory like those that remain after any of life's unforgettable contacts. There only remains my attempt to articulate the pleasure in examining the ingredients of the loaf and the quiet joy in the hyacinth; I can say of my life experiences to my grandchildren, "I have sailed in a felucca on the Nile, seen the Mona Lisa, watched sunrise at Machu Picchu, and taken tea at the Savoy."

# *The Albert*
# *Piccadilly Hotel*
# *Brown Hotel*
# *The Grill at the Cafe Royal*
# *Palm Room at the Ritz*

London's many hyacinths are both ordinary and extraordinary, but each supplies its own perfume that creates the aromatic blend which surrounds any experience there among the loaves. At first we stayed at a Bed and Breakfast with Mrs. Mabel Pierce, a piano teacher, in Ealing Common. Later, we were hosted by Pete and JoAnn Jennings, Oklahomans and personal friends of Lavonn and Norma Brown. Employees of Halliburton, they had been London

residents for sixteen years. Her parents were members of Norma's and
Lavonn's church, which precipitated Pete's nickname for Norma: VW
for Vicar's Wife. So I promptly dubbed her SM-VW: Sergeant Major-
Vicar's Wife, as balance to my euphemistic double title, NA, Navigator-Archivist, which also provided us with an equal number of syl-
lables, very important for our egalitarian quest. As our acquaintence
developed, I learned Pete came from Wynnewood, the town of my
birth, and had known my grandfather. Further, his brother is Jim
Jennings, my friend from a writing class, who was a vice president
and legal counsel at Liberty National Bank in Oklahoma City. Their
generosity extended to loaning us their car for our tea trek and a key
to their lovely flat in Harley House on Marylebone Road for use
during our London stops. Because of his work, they had lived in many
different places, including Iran, and own many beautiful antiques.
Their flat looked just as a London flat should.

The trips in and out of London gave us several opportunities to
roam that wonderful city and sample book shops, points of interest
(we visited the Domesday Exhibit, census of William the Conqueror
in its ninth centenary celebration), and the theatre. We savored The
British Museum and verified tea information at The Victoria and
Albert Museum. I particularly relished the Museum Library Galleries
where I could stand, mouth agape, I fear, in front of dozens of price-
less treasures: four gospels in Latin, written and illuminated about 800
at Charlemagne's court; Latin gospels written and illuminated in St.
Augustine's Abbey the second half of the 8th century; Bede's Life of
St. Cuthbert written and illuminated at Durham in the late 12th
century; Book of Hours in Latin of Queen Elizabeth, dated 1420;
letters written by Edmund Spenser, John Donne, Andrew Marvell,
Daniel Defoe; Francis Bacon's memo book; John Milton's Common-
place Book of Notes on Political and Domestic Subjects; Thomas

Gray's 1750 "Elegy Written in a Country Churchyard;" John Keats's "Hyperion;" Charlotte Bronte's 1847 *Jane Eyre;* the only known autograph of S.T. Coleridge's "Kubla Khan;" Pope Innocent III's Bull to King John, granting him England; the Magna Carta.

Once, after a luxurious continental breakfast at the Hyde Park Hotel, we chanced upon the "Household Cavalry" of the Queen going to another part of the park for one of their two annual inspections. When we visited The National Gallery, I sat and wept before the beauty of the Constable, Gainesborough, and Turner paintings.

I especially enjoyed watching people at the book shops. One particular gentleman caught my imagination while I stared after him as he left. Impeccably groomed, his morning costume was both complete and replete with cane, bowler hat, and pink boutonniere. I compared him with a man I had observed in the train on our way downtown. He, too, was well-groomed, but had "porch roof" eyebrows, looking waxed, standing out as far as the brim of his hat. What was my point? Just the observation and the comment on it. Henry James wrote in *English Hours* of cushion words between American and English readers, "All a writer must do is observe—comment." However, for this observer-commentator, I have the crusader's dilemma. The transition from crusader to commentator is a difficult turn to negotiate. My pilgrimage with my Puritan strains have created some tensions about unstrapping from the guilt when the crusader harness is dropped. The benefits correct the imbalance, though, with all that is gained with the loss of the narrow crusader perspective.

On one outing, we took a double-decker downtown along Oxford Street while I wildly tried to sort the surging evocations of events and literary reference I had read about that area. Norma, SM-VW, took me, NA, to her favorite china shop and taught me to buy a proper tea service. As a result, I proudly own a tea set for six in Worcester Contessa (cups, saucers, 9-inch plates, one large plate, pitcher, cream, and sugar)—and six 6-inch plates in Worcester Howard— same white with a royal blue band). Then, I dutifully followed her to Fortnum & Mason's for a proper tea strainer, listening intently to her explanation of precise tea preparation, much as Magnum would attend to Higgins from the Magnum PI television series.

Usually, we took the tube back, and I loved that as well, for we exited on Baker Street, where Arthur Conan Doyle located Sherlock Holmes in his fictional lodgings. On the way up the escalator, a tile wall has numerous Holmes silhouettes. A short walk from the exit took us to the Jennings flat. A block from Harley House, at the corner of Marylebone High and Marylebone Road, was once 1 Devonshire Terrace, a home of Charles Dickens. A bas relief of characters from the six works he wrote while living in that spot circles the building and continues around the side, with the legend, "On this site stood 1 Devonshire Terrace. Charles Dickens lived here from 1839-1851." A quotation from the great man, himself, completes the memorial plaque: "'I seem as if I had plucked myself out of my proper soil when I left 1 Devonshire Terrace and could take root no more until I return to it.' — Charles Dickens." A sacred spot for a literature professor who has a specialization in nineteenth-century British fiction!!

Down the road, behind Marylebone Parish Church, which is built now on the spot of 1 Devonshire Terrace, stands a garden and old grave markers from the first parish church. Charles Wesley is buried there. The spot also holds a monument to his wife, Sarah, and their son, Charles, and a Samuel Wesley. Charles died March 29, 1788, at 80, and Sarah, 22 December 1822, at 96. A sacred spot for a devotee of the church and Christian history!

Always up and off by 7:30 a.m. to Victoria Station via the tube, the sights and sounds on the train held me transfixed: school girls with Cockney accents in gray wool uniforms with pleated dark skirts, lighter blazers and sweaters with patterned blouses that had CCH embroidered in blue on blazer pocket (one was doing home-work that had some allusion to the Bible while saying she had "a fight at the chip shop" as her friend was eating M&Ms); the min-gling of the voices with the train's click-bump; reading people, typified by one section of two facing seats, where one man was absorbed in the sports section of the paper, a bearded black man in an enormous green tam stared at a book written in a language I did not recognize, and the man beside him sat engrossed in a paperback edition of *Othello*; station names such as Hammersmith and Uxbridge; red brick buildings with slate roofs, chimney pots, and an occasional TV antenna at a precarious angle; scudding gray clouds shading the blue in the sky; trees in both new leaf and bare branches; a passing train that blotted out all; rail lines bunched like flower stems; a church spire thrusting up a finger to test the wind; all sights shut out by descent; and the seeming antiquity of it all. Victoria could have awakened and seen it that morning without surprise, but a jet to my left made it contemporary—Victoria is gone.

During our rambles about London, at various times, we break-fasted at The Albert, had morning coffee at The Piccadilly Hotel, lunched at The Cafe Royal, took tea at the Brown Hotel and high tea in the Palm Room of the Ritz. To reach The Albert, we walked from Victoria Station. Called Victorian survival, the restaurant presents the ultimate in Victorian decor: dark woods, etched glass, dark bannisters of stairs, and dark reds and black relieved by gold in the carpet. All about the stairwell hang pictures of famous people: Harold McMillan (1957-63), Anthony Eden (1955-57),

Clement Atlee (1945-51), a large one of Churchill, and a huge portrait of Victoria, to mention a few of them. A sign out front said, "Now serving traditional breakfast." We walked in and were sent upstairs.

Through a glass foyer at the top of the stairs with tiny paned glass in the doors, we entered the dining room. A coal fire flickered on the grate, back of a polished brass hearth and fire tools. Dark wood tables surrounded by red velvet upholstered chairs waited invitingly. Seated, I stared about. An intriguing piece of furniture was the service bar or sideboard. I asked the waitress what it was called and she said, "Dumb waiter, you know, — stupid." I hope she was using "stupid" as an adjective and not a noun. On a high pedestal extending from its backboard sat a plant; the "'stupid' waiter" also included a leaded glass backboard or back splash. A "traditional English breakfast" comprised coffee, toast, egg, sausage, bacon, and oatmeal (which we asked to substitute for cereal from "full olde English breakfast"). On the wall was a framed napkin that belonged to Victoria; above, the ceiling boasted gilt bas reliefs in fan shapes; maroon velvet with tie backs and swagged top draped the windows. The episode was a leisurely, "loverly" way to begin a day. In the words of SM-VW, "For what has been, thanks. For what is to be, yes."

I have never had morning coffee in greater elegance than that encountered at the Piccadilly Hotel's Lounge. Rose on rose mingled with some shades of blue covered the large, stuffed furniture, and repeated from coffee tables "set" in off-white china with rose colored flowers. Gilt bas reliefs of musical instruments on pinkish-brown walls with lighter ceiling borders in Wedgewood-like shells and feathers hovered over us. A harp leaned in a corner to my right near an Oriental screen. The room was square on three sides, but oval on the fourth, with four chest high pedestals holding oriental vases and ferns and making the room square by their line on the floor. Four huge chandeliers repeated the feather/shell patterns in their crystal. On the right, French doors of mirrors reflected other glass doors opposite revealing a beautiful restaurant, The Oak Room, which appeared from The Lounge as a duplicate dining room in the mirrors. Our waiter told me the wood was Australian oak, new, made to look like the older outfittings of The Lounge. That reminder of shared colonial connections kneaded Australia into my London loaf by means of the Piccadilly Lounge hyacinth.

The morning we found The Cafe Royal, a meeting place of the literati in the earlier 1900s, we decided to return for lunch. Selecting lamb for two in The Grill Room, we settled back in red velvet and gilt chairs, basking in self-assumed importance, knowing we were eating in the same place people like D.H. Lawrence, James Whistler, Oscar Wilde, J.B. Priestley, Greer Garson, Sinclair Lewis, T.S. Eliot, Pavlova, and Edward VIII and George VI (as princes) had dined. Heavily rococo and massively ornate in gilt, red and maroon velvet, and wall-hangings with gilt-fringed swags, giving a window effect, the room was overwhelming and hard to absorb. We noted the perfectly English couple having lunch (taking all courses, and she, making-up her face later), and next to them, two men and one woman with papers spread and talking over a business lunch. No one seemed aware of murals in walls and ceilings, wall mirrors, nudes above each wall grouping of three lamps, hanging long wreaths about themselves, and hoisting urns above their heads. Maybe we became more metropolitan as the lunch casually continued, but we agree to this day that the ultimate in style and flair is to be served lunch by *three* men in black cutaways. On days when I feel dowdy or unappreciated, I recall the exquisite aroma of that hyacinth from its literary loaf.

*Palm Court Tea Room — London Ritz*

After some time trying to find Ramsgate, where I wanted to locate an 18th-century gathering place of writers (I could not remember if it was nearer Blackfriars Bridge or Tower Bridge—it was the latter), we went to tea at The Brown Hotel after a turn around magnificent St. Paul's to soothe my ruffled aestheticism. The Brown worked its magic with its understated grandeur and dominant stained glass. The clientele aided the aura. Two women sat over "set tea," one in a large fur hat with her fur coat across the chair arm, and the other with black swinging bangs, engaged in animated conversation. I found one couple striking, arresting; he had the pink English skin with the right amount of cuff showing below his coat sleeve, and she kept pushing back black hair cut one length that continued falling about her beautiful Oriental face. Her black stockings, shoes, and skirt, with fuschia silk shirt, made her skin whiter.

In our American all weather-coats and sensible walking shoes, we tried to assume an English guise as we joined the rhythm of taking tea from the lovely service on a cream and rose ringed Wedgewood pattern with heavy silver and brown linen napkins, snug by a coal fire on a grate. Somehow, The Brown's retained fragrance emanates from a mental image of a fur casually tossed and black, black hair surrounding a perfect white face.

On a day reserved to do all we had not yet accomplished on our London lists, we accepted the inevitable; we had to give up walking, subways, and buses, and go in the London cabs (which was, after all, on our "To Do" list). Late in the day, we struck off for The Ritz to try having high tea, but not assured we could, because reservations are required. Our luck held. A party for the second sitting did not show, and we were given their table.

The only comparison for high tea at The Ritz Palm Room is
The Savoy Thames Foyer; each goes beyond experience to become
event. After all, Cesar Ritz, the founder, was the first hotel manager at The Savoy. However, in spite of their similarities, striking
differences do exist. Where the Thames Foyer projects British
countryside and subdued English manners, the Palm Room evokes
a classic quality and a busy formality. Three steps up from the
foyer to the Palm Court, flanked by Corinthian columns, beige/
brown marble repeated in the floor is covered by four carpets
reproducing the rose and beige in floral patterns. Victorian and
French influence also abound in carved, white enameled furniture,
and chairs which appear both Victorian and French. From The
Palm Court, looking back to the entrance and foyer, we could see a
baby grand piano (the source of the music for tea) and a series of
gilt mirrors on all walls of the foyer and the Palm Court. The result
created its own luxurious hall-of-mirrors effect and reflected the
unmistakable Victorian style in chandeliers comprised of lamps
which were duplicated on the walls in four groupings at either end.
The *maitre d,'* assisted by waiters in black, who had assistants in
white jackets, served from blue and white Royal Doulton and
heavy silver. Pink damask cloth and napkins (embroidered "The
Ritz") completed the presentation. While munching cucumber
sandwiches, scones with clotted-cream, and elaborate tea cakes, we
could only observe with admiration the casual manner in which a
couple of young women, 18 or 19, and two 30-ish women in front
of us and to the right, participated matter-of-factly in that cultural
ceremony of high tea. Bemused, we noted one couple and an
interchange between the gentleman and the head waiter with the
air of authority in the man and the *maitre d's* attitude of automatic
servility, another evidence of British aristocratic manners.

When I recount that list of my life's loaves and hyacinths to my grandchildren ("I have sailed in a felucca on the Nile, seen the Mona Lisa, watched sunrise at Machu Picchu, and taken tea at the Savoy"), I will need to add, "Oh, and also at The Ritz."

*Auntie's Tea Room — Cambridge*

# II.

# Loaves and Hyacinths in the Fens

## ⇢⇒ *Cambridge* ⇐⇠
## *Auntie's Tea Room*

Auntie's Tea Room snuggles between shops across the street from King's College. With decor in green and white, tables sit beneath white lace covering green and white print cloths. Cane bottomed bentwood chairs hover by the tables on green and black carpet. Wall sconces, uniformed waitresses in black with white aprons, gilt wall mirrors, and Victorian photographs complete the ambiance. Cream teas, with egg and cucumber sandwiches, scones, cream, jam, and butter, disappear into the congenial atmosphere to an accompaniment of lively chatter. Young and old enjoy Auntie's. Mature couples sit by the broad picture window framing Market Hill, while students, some of them internationals, sip and chat in recessed areas. A young man beneath a corner shadow box with miniatures of flowers, places his motorcycle helmet on the table, and orders tea.

Auntie's location gives it triple blossom value as a hyacinth. Yet its clientele sit quietly, taking tea, seeming to be oblivious to the soaring spires at King's Chapel, in view, with its cornerstone laid by Henry VI's builders in 1446, where Peter Paul Rubens's "Adoration of the Magi" graces the altar and Ann Boleyn's initials are in the screen. The tea drinkers show no awareness of Trinity College, a few hundred paces up King's Parade, which becomes Trinity Street in front of the college, where mute architecture witnesses eloquently to historical fact. And after a while, the visitor's sensitivities synchronize with the tea room's rhythm, and tend, also, to accept more casually the quintessential character of the surroundings as setting for Auntie's. But memory nudges to recall Trinity where Lord Byron bathed naked in the fountain, and kept a bear, because students could not have a dog. At the same college, closer to the backs where punts skim on the Cam, is Wren's magnificent library and Nevile's Court below it where Newton measured the speed of sound the first time. A visitor can do the same thing by standing on the Court's west end, stamping a foot, and hearing the clear sharp echo.

Two blocks to the right of Auntie's is Christ's College with John Milton's ancient Mulberry, fragile in its huge mound, under which the poet supposedly sat as a student to compose "Lycidas" to lament the death of a young friend. At Magdalene College, left from Auntie's and beyond Trinity, is the Pepys Library, 3000 volumes bound for the diarist in the late 1600s, standing exactly as he housed them in his own library. Samuel Pepys bequeathed them to his college for posterity.

Completely relaxed, Auntie's patrons scarcely notice either the cassock-clad priest on the sidewalk, talking earnestly and gesticulating with a student, or an older woman on a bicycle, zipping past the two, with back-pack filled and her gray hair enlivened by a broad Kelly green stripe flowing through it.

Fed by Auntie's fare, the mind goes to the loaf that is East Anglia. Beginning at the Thames estuary, East Anglia balloons into the North Sea, encasing Essex, Suffolk, Norfolk, and Cambridgeshire in its boundaries. From the south, Essex and Suffolk wool villages with their majestic Medieval churches, subscribed and supported in their day like contemporary rival football teams in this one, advance toward Cambridgeshire and Norfolk where topography divides as did Caesar's Gaul into three parts: the Fens, the Brecks, and the Broads. The Fens are the island areas that existed in a great swamp lake created by four rivers running through a level expanse to the Wash, an inland arm of the North Sea that is bordered by Norfolk on the east and Cambridgeshire on the south. Low tide produces as much as seven miles of sand from the shore. With the marshland nearer the ocean being higher, the Fens were isolated at high tide. Land reclamation began first with windmills, using Holland's methodologies. Active drainage commenced in the seventeenth century. Power for pumping from the lower level land to the higher rivers progressed from steam, to diesel, to electricity.

The Broads, to the east on the North Sea side, are a series of lagoons and waterways with connections between six rivers. Origins of the lakes, or meres as they are called, shrouded themselves in mystery until persistent investigation revealed them as peat diggings from late Saxon and early Roman times. With the difference between land and water levels measured in inches, flat East Anglia in the Broads can appear to be grazing sheep and coasting boats side by side.

The Breckland bridges the Fens and the Broads. Once called East Anglia's desert, it is rich in fertile sandy loam over chalk and flint. Devoted to the sheep industry of the Middle Ages and destroyed by the animals, Breckland is now dedicated to pheasant, pines, and military uses.

Cambridge opens the door to East Anglia. As the nearest point to London on the Fenland waterway network, it evolved from being a low ford of the River Cam at first. With the Fens and the Wash to the north, and swamps to the south, it was an inland port and transport center for the Romans. A border town for the Kingdoms of East Anglia, Middle Anglia, and Mercia, Cambridge developed into a battle staging area for the Normans during the Conquest. In *Little Domesday*, we had seen in London William's survey of Essex, Norfolk, Suffolk at the penultimate compilation stage of his census, after the information was assembled, proved in court, and copied. In 1211, King John chartered its annual fair, called Stourbridge Fair. Already established as a shipping portage and by-pass to London from northern England by avoiding the dangerous sea journey around East Anglia, Cambridge became home to the famous fair by accident. Cloth merchants en route to Norich had their goods drenched by a rain storm while crossing the Cam. They spread their wares to dry, and promptly sold all they had. The annual fair was the result.

A center of learning emerged in Cambridge on the banks of the Cam. Early in the thirteenth century, a well-developed university organization thrived. The first college gained a charter in 1281, and each century since has passed its colleges into the system, changing the world with Cambridge-educated minds. John Milton and Charles Darwin went to Christ's College. William Wordsworth studied at St. John's. A clergyman from Emmanuel, John Harvard, emigrated to the New World in 1636 and died at thirty-one, bequeathing half his estate and 320 books to found a college in Massachusetts, naming its town for his university's. Newton gave a working foundation to modern science. Today's surgical miracles date to William Harvey's discovery of blood circulation. Bacon's philosophy of law permeates every court room. Auntie's, the lovely hyacinth, sits on a fertile grain bed for a vast variety of loaves.

## ⊸⇒ *Cambridge* ⇐⊷
## *The Copper Kettle*

Farther down King's Parade, toward Queen's College, is another style of tea room. The Copper Kettle, a multi-purpose tea shop that serves coffee in the morning and lunches at noon, offers tea from a different stage than Auntie's. Scholarship is in its oxygen. The university mood is almost stereotypical: dark wood, nearly black tables and chairs, black and red carpet. Though a pram rests in the doorway, and somewhere a baby cries, academia sits at tea. Beams, bed warmers on the wall, and a high shelf displaying blue and white plates contribute to its Tudor flavor. A large round-faced pendulum schoolhouse clock marks The Copper Kettle propriety.

A gray-haired man with a limp so severe he can hardly walk, stops at the table and asks, "You've got your plans for Cambridge?"

"Yes."

"Nice day for walking." He hobbles away.

Neither he nor the other tea drinkers seem to be aware that Erasmus hovers above his own Queen's College across the courtyards, and Cromwell's spirit diapproves the students punting on the backs while sipping wine from crystal stems. Why should they? A present fed by the past endures for enjoyment. Only hyacinth and loaf inspectors analyze it.

*The Old Fire Engine House — Ely*

# ~== *Ely* ==~
## *Old Fire Station*

Ely lies 16 miles north of Cambridge. Its Cathedral rises across the Fens like a fairy castle, growing to an enormity that dwarfs the one who approaches. A short walk from its West Tower, and facing a small church called St. Mary the Virgin contiguous to the Cathedral green, stands the Old Fire Engine House. Having been what its name says, the building today continues as an art gallery on the upper levels and a tea shop on the lower floor and in the gardens. Old describes as well as defines. Uneven stone floors, part in squares of red and yellow, and part in smaller brick-size yellow, warm the dining room. Unmatched antique benches, chairs, and tables, one of which needs a place mat under a leg to level it, surround a serving table holding cakes, scones, and tea biscuits. A bay window framed by russet floral drapes, evoking a Pennsylvania Dutch feeling, opens onto the garden, making its white wrought iron tables, shrubs, and perfectly symmetrical tulips and daffodils participants in the dining room ambiance. Contributing their own charm, amateur looking paintings complete with flourished signatures hang beneath individual focus lamps which light them professionally.

A gray-haired man wearing a clerical collar dressed in a black shirt, tan pants and sweater, and gray coat sits by the bay window overlooking the garden. A girl bringing three fresh daffodils in a small pottery vase says to him, "You're early. I've not had time to beautify."

Two young men enter, one with dark hair, the other with ruddy cheeks, and step to the kitchen door. "May we have some coffee, please?" the dark-haired one calls, emphasizing coffee.

Flower Girl answers, "It's in there."

Ruddy Cheeks replies, "It's looking all sadly empty, I'm afraid."

They choose a table near the outside door with the key in the keyhole, opened to the garden where bed flowers guard the wall base beyond and the bird calls sound louder than the few dull car noises on the front street. In an aqua shirt that makes his face more pink, Ruddy Cheeks announces, "I have to read Lord Byron." Then he stands. "Bisquit is all we need?"

Dark Hair nods. "Quite."

A man and woman join Cleric. Husband asks, "Where's your friend?"

Cleric raises his eyebrows. "Don't know."

"I'm so used to seeing you together."

"Lovely day, isn't it?" Cleric sips. "Have you seen a swallow yet? Or heard a cuckoo?"

"I've seen a swallow, but not a cuckoo." Husband munches. "How long have you been retired? Ten years?"

"Yes. Good time of life. Yes. Yes." The Cathedral's West Tower looks like a launch-poised rocket behind him.

"Do you come here every day?"

"Yes. Yes."

Ruddy Cheeks returns once again to the service table and looks toward Dark Hair. "More of these?"

A self-guided tour results from following the changing floor designs of the Old Fire Engine House. Over the mantel, a huge photograph shows the front of the building back of a turn-of-the-century horse-drawn fire wagon, posed fire brigade, and harnessed horse ready to run. Stone in the tea room gives way to wood parquet in the house, succeeded by carpet on the stairs and second floor with floor levels staggered at landings, giving an impression of one room being a third floor. The galleries are there, with the one uppermost accommodating a show of nude paintings. A vicar of Ely, Cleric from downstairs, comes in to study them intently.

Ely. Its name stems from religion-based legend. When St. Dunstan, insistent on a celibate priesthood, visited the island area in the Fens, he encountered priests who were married, or needed to be. He changed them into eels. The story accounted for the eels that abounded in the area and described the island by name. Eel Island eventually became Isle of Ely, and, finally, with drainage of the Fens and loss of island characteristics, it was simply Ely.

Queen Etheldreda founded it as a religious center. Born near Newmarket in Exning, a palace of East Anglian Wuffinga kings, Etheldreda was the daughter of King Anna. She lived in a castle full of saintly sisters, and she wanted to take holy orders. But King Anna married her off to a British prince, Tonbert, lord of the wild Celtic Gervii tribe in the Fens before getting himself killed by the pagan Mercians in a battle at Blythborough. Etheldreda would not consummate her marriage, and her husband's death left her with his Fenland possessions which included the Isle of Ely. Another political marriage, to Egfrid, King of Northumberland, fell her lot in 671, but Etheldreda remained true to her call and virginity, the two being synonymous for the holy life. Denied his wife's conjugal intimacy, Egfrid permitted her to visit an aunt who was an abbess, another of the holy women in her family. Once there, she received the veil from Bishop Wilfreid of York, and poor Egrid never had another chance

*Pilgrim's Parlour Tea Room*

at his wife's virginity, fortified as it was by Holy Mother Church. Valiently, he chased her purity back and forth across the Fenlands. He almost caught her once, but high tide on Ely Island kept her chastity safe. Relieved, Etheldreda thrust her staff into the ground and it rooted. Recognizing the omen (and perhaps the symbolism), she started a nunnery, ran it, and eventually administered a monastery as well, maintaining her cherished state of virtue all the while. But, alas, she died of a throat cancer, reportedly because of her frivolous love for necklaces when she was a little girl. Her holy sister Sexburgh (no comment) assumed control of the establishment and had Etheldreda's remains buried in the chapel. When miracles occurred, Etheldreda's importance grew, and eventually she was canonized. Her name shortened to St. Audrey, and fairs were held in her name where trinkets like St. Audrey's necklaces were sold. The word "tawdry" came from junk sold at the fairs.

Historically, control of the old Anglo-Saxon saints was important. The Danes, in particular, would steal their remains. Etheldreda was once carried across the river at Brandon, but came home at last, pure as ever. After the Danish onslaughts, a Benedictine Abbey arose in 970 in Ely. With the Conquest in 1066, the town was a stronghold for Anglo-Saxon resistance under command of Hereward the Wake. William went there in the process of the Conquest, and finally, the Normans controlled Ely. Their presence is marked by the beginning of the church in 1083, a Cathedral since the time of Henry I, with Norman architecture in evidence throughout its buildings. Its Octagon, or high lantern, has carvings of the Etheldreda escapades on the corbels. In the *Domesday* Exhibit in Chancery Lane, we read a survey of the Abbey of Ely estates that showed the questions the Domesday commissioners asked: What is the name of the manor? Who held it in the time of King Edward (before the Conquest)?

Who holds it now? How many hides? Plough teams (for tax)? Villeins? Cottars? Slaves? Freemen? While I was never far removed from my awareness of the Anglo-Saxon beginnings and the seafaring effects on this island kingdom, I often recalled my laborious efforts with Old English and translation of the Anglo-Saxon chronicles. In *Domesday*, as casually as one might mention the daily newspaper events, the Chronicle of 1085 was presented. Ely, Ely, how modern you are in your antiquity.

## ⤙═ *Ely* ═⤚
## *Pilgrim's Parlour*

In full sight of the Cathedral, Pilgrim's Parlour Tea Room sits opposite both it and St. Mary's Church in another direction. It looks onto St. Mary's green where Oliver Cromwell drilled his squads and sent threatening messages to Cathedral authorities. He came from St. Ives to Ely to live to assume his grandfather's position of Steward for the Dean and Chapter of Ely. Responsible for collecting a tenth of all produce in the region, Cromwell was in charge of the "tythe-barn." He once led his men into the Cathedral during Communion to rout the papists, as he termed the Church of England clergy, but refrained from the destruction which he later unleashed on other cathedral sites during the Civil War. Even Ely Cathedral did not escape damage later in the fighting.

Appropriately, Pilgrim's Parlour Tea Room has an Early American look. Or, is it late English? Unpainted chairs, a hutch at the back with dishes and a display of wares, with a Wedgewood vase on the top shelf, prints of Ely Cathedral on the wall, and a framed bit of poetry from Langland's *Piers Plowman* about "ploughmen" in February decorate it. A wonderful wooden cut-out of a teapot hangs in the window. Coming with pad in hand, a waitress brings tea in an all white service, except for a green stripe around the top of the teapot. The menu reads, "Tea: freshly cut sandwiches, ham or cheese; cream tea, two scones with jam and cream." Wall lamps with floral etchings on their globes, and skirted table in green, white and red print look Victorian, but do not detract from the Pilgrim impact. However, the effect created by sitting with a view of the Cathedral out the window grounds the setting in historical reality that assumes dominance.

A woman and a boy come in, order, and have a discussion about music. Theirs is a teacher-student relationship. She talks to him about a performance two weeks away, looking over her glasses at him all the while. "You'll do fine," she says, dispensing with instructions, and turning to tea.

Etheldreda's heritage seems obvious across the greens of the two churches, with the smaller one echoing Cromwell's commands for imaginative visitors. Two descendent daughters of the ancient queen's spiritual sisters who did not regard celibacy so rigidly sit in the Pilgrim Parlour, appropriately, being American offshoots of the spiritual tree, and bask in both Etheldreda's ancestral strength and that of Cromwell's. The tithes that make Ely's loaf bring them to the Old Engine Fire House and Pilgrim's Parlour—hyacinths both.

## ⇢⇒ *King's Lynn* ⇐⇠
## *Riverside Restaurant*

King's Lynn, another town in the Fens with an exotic name, holds within its walls St. George's Guildhall where Shakespeare's company once played (and was paid NOT to play in an "outburst of

beastly puritanism"). Armed with information that King's Lynn is
the only place in England where Shakespeare possibly, or likely,
played a part himself, we had a mission to find the theater and the
Riverside Restaurant and Crofters Coffee House under it. Viewing
numerous castles and gaining sensitivity to language codes for our
own shorthand gave us a name for our car: The Keep. Castle Keeps
are the principal fortification areas, the most secure part of the sites,
and the place where the most important people of the social units
stay for protection. After Ely, we entered our "keep" and turned it in
the direction of King's Lynn. Our consistent strategy upon entering
a town took us on a search to find "town centre" and the "information centre." The two are not synonymous. One provided a
geographical orientation, and the other, if we had good fortune,
granted maps, leaflets, and instructions. We could usually find the
former, but rarely the latter. And if we did, for a variety of plausible
and implausible reasons, it would not be open.

Snug in The Keep, we found town centre—Saturday Market
between St. Margaret's Church and the Guildhall, which is again a
theater and currently the location of The Fermoy Center where the
Riverside Restaurant and Crofters Coffee House, indeed, carry on
business under the theater. We even found a Car Park, and commissioned The Keep to guard our possessions while we sallied out on
errand as the ancient knights would leave their keeps. The theater
was locked. We could not find an authority or key to allow entrance,
but we went around back to the stage door entrance and walked
quietly with great depth of emotion through a passage with overhead
beams whitened by age.

The restaurant is in a "cellar" location with the dining room in a
barrel-vaulted brick enclosure. Upholstered benches run the length
either side with woven seats, wrought iron tables, and bentwood

chairs opposite the benches. Double wall lamps behind on the benches's walls, above a tile shelf formed with the bench backs, grant illumination. Two chandeliers of five like lamps were at the entrance half of the area, making a dim but pleasant interior. At the cash register end, by the stairs, a large gilt antique wall mirror remained like a sentinel, both containing and expanding the space. Dark green carpet, plants at the opposite end lighted with a plant light, and an immaculate service of Wedgewood in a white Insignia pattern maintained a quiet elegance. The menu offered a selection of cakes, pastries, and lunch fare with teas like Crofters House Blend, Ceylon Orange Pekoe, Darjeeling, Fine Assam, and Earl Grey. (We had Darjeeling.)

Playbills lined part of the wall: *My Fair Lady*, *Fiddler on the Roof*, and *Desert Song*, to name a few. The place has the look of antiquity, but the top part of the vault reveals a more recent construction than the initial walls. We indulged in a series of likely reasons for why there were six very old iron rings in the ceiling, wondering if they had anything to do with the "outburst of beastly puritanism." Waitresses dressed in black skirts, white blouses, and white ruffled aprons. A young Peter Ustinov look-a-like sat next to us, reading. Animated art talk sounded from our left.

". . . I said he could do the reading . . ."

Retracing to town centre (Saturday Market between St. Margaret's Church and the Guildhall), we discovered market was in full swing, since we were there on a Saturday. The place has been a market for centuries, with records from 1427 saying Jews could no longer sell meat in Jew's Lane unless it "be near the church," in order to get revenue from it. St. Margaret's did receive a cannon shot from the other side of the river, the Great Ouse, when Cromwell bom-

*The Lavender Fields — Caley Mills Tea Room*

barded the city. King's Lynn was Royalist during the Civil War, though as the great trade center, it would logically not have been. The Guildhall is a flint and freestone chequer-board looking building built in 1421. Today it houses King John's regalia inside, since he stayed in Lynn. Near the end of his life, while he feasted, his treasure chest was lost as it was crossing the river. He died shortly thereafter. A display exhibits a complete set of charters from his time, and one from Canute. On the Guildhall is this information: "Hall of the Holy and Undivided Trinity, built in 1422 on earlier foundations, it has a stone floor. The arms of Elizabeth I and James I are over the entrance porch. Assembly rooms were added in 1767, it was used as a town hall until 1695 when the adjoining building was occupied. In the regalia room are displayed the King John cup, the Red Register, which is the oldest paper book in the world, a unique collection of charters, a sword of state and four maces."

Going down Queen's Street toward King's Street, which it becomes, we saw old ships on a back wash and oil-circled water below us where a dozen swans, one of them with six little ones, were swimming. We stopped in to visit Clifton House, a combination ancient warehouse and merchant's house, which ran down to the river. Those fresh-faced English mothers with babies in prams walked by; one passing me had put an eyelet dust maid cap on her sleeping little one. We passed King's Staithe Square (wharf) and an OLD sailing ship, riding high in the mud.

Delighted with the place, we retraced to The Keep and headed to Castle Rising for a cultural side-trip. An old Norman castle with Saxon and Roman history, regal in its ruins and smug inside its dry moat, it sits in its lawn atop a high mound overlooking the countryside. I read about Castle Rising in *Domesday*, and remembered the account when I stood on the ramparts of the castle ruins, its features still remarkably intact. *Domesday* says of Castle Rising, "A large village of 250 inhabitants, Castle Rising was held by Odo, Bishop of Bayeaux, the Conqueror's half-brother and one of the most powerful men in Domesday, England. And in addition to 1 outlying estate, RISING (Risinga), 3 ploughlands, then as now, 12 villeins and 39 borders, then 4 serfs, no 3.14 acres of meadow . . ." I stood and looked at all that as did the Domesday surveyor. But land and stone outlasted all of them, as they will endure my sojourn. Castle Rising's position deemed that it went from hand to hand: 1331-56, Queen Isabella was kept there by her son, Edward III, for suspicion of complicity in his father's murder; the Black Prince held it; Richard II owned it. Now it is in the hands of the Howard family. As we pulled in our own drawbridge doors at our Keep, we agreed that our King's Lynn loaf finds its yeast in the historical importance of the area; our hyacinth bloomed from the Guildhall with the theater and Crofters Coffee House beneath it. A special fragrance wafted from the wispy contact with Shakespeare across the centuries. Although we looked in vain for his initials scratched in the beams beneath the theater, we feel certain he walked that way for his curtain call.

## ⟜⟝ *Heacham* ⟞⟜
### *Caley Mills Tea Room*

English lavender comes from the Fens and is exported worldwide. Caley Mills, with its Tea Room, is found in Heacham in the midst of the Lavender Fields. The mill and house are approached across a lavender field from the highway. We trekked around lavender beds with their names like "Nana Alba," "Royal Purple," "Midas," and "Deb's Delight" on little markers. Built about 1810 of local Carr stone, the mill was used until 1923 as a water mill. No longer a working mill, the parts remain in place. The mill race is at the north end with the wheel which drove the grinding machinery on the first floor of the building. Upper floors today serve for storage and offices. The old miller's cottage remains as the tea room. Inside the tea room, whitewashed walls oblige as a gallery with photos of lavender harvests on them. Appearing larger because of its open-beamed ceiling, the room is about 20 by 45 feet with the fireplace doubling as a divider between the serving and dining areas. Over it hangs an enormous framed drawing of the lavender plant with "Mattioli Venice, 1565" printed on its mat. Beyond the tea room, at the outside back, a tent-covered area provided for outdoor eating and, in the front, tables stood for garden service. Hinged, paned windows had pottery urns and pitchers in them. Five doors led from the shop: two to the front, two to the back, and one to the tent room. Glass and stainless tableware waited on mats with a Victorian print. Small pottery vases held fresh flowers. Our table didn't have one, so we took a vase from another table. The furniture had an "Early American" look, but the Caley Mills Tea Room, although in a miller's house, delightful and pleasant, was not antique in its decor. Everything—from the floral print curtains at the windows to the Dudson blue and white tableware—matched. After seeing blue and white dishes all over East Anglia, this was the first time we ate from it.

English voices were loud. The Caley Mills Tea Room served social interchange as well as tea. Two tables of older women, most of them gray-haired, joined each other. They laughed and talked boisterously, like teenagers.

"Teresa's not been well all week . . ."

" . . . go to the doctor . . ."

" . . . come off it! I'm younger than you!"

*Tea in the Garden*

" . . . I had two sinus infections . . . and now this morning . . . "

At another table, a grandmother showed her grandson, about seven, how to fold a paper hat from a napkin while his bemused mother looked on.

Back at the clinic at the next table:

" . . . poor circulation . . . "

" . . . I was coming from the coach . . . "

"His wife's a labor counselor . . . "

The staff carried trays, heavy when loaded, to the tables for the old ladies. One, the last woman to enter, obviously a stroke victim, had an affected left side.

After tea, we dutifully went to the gift shop to buy booklets and a few lavender gifts to take home. Lavender does not dominate the market at Caley Mills. Herbs like bellflower, wild marjoram, yarrow, and foxglove are available. Their names seem to be the most exotic thing about them.

Loaf? What can be more sturdy than English voices and the exuberant conversation of these civilized, polite people? The sound alone convinces a hearer that the sun, of course, will be up on time in the morning. Hyacinth? Lavender, of course; it holds Empire in its fragrance. Add lavender, Victorian decor, and an airy, bright tea room in a miller's cottage: hyacinths, all!

The Anna Sewell Tea Shoppe

# III.

# Loaves and Hyacinths in the Broads

## ⇥ *Great Yarmouth* ⇤
## *The Anna Sewell Tea Shoppe*

The Anna Sewell Tea Shoppe operates from the ground floor of the house in Great Yarmouth where Anna Sewell, author of *Black Beauty*, and her family lived. Yarmouth, a trade and business city, benefits from its position in The Broads, the series of lagoons and waterways which connect East Anglia's six rivers, and its location on the east North Sea side. The difference between land and water levels is minuscule, so while we traversed The Broads, from a distance we often had the sense that water vehicles mysteriously moved through grass. In literature, Yarmouth's 19th-century eternal life comes at the hand of Charles Dickens, because it is where David Copperfield goes to Peggotty's family, and Steerforth betrays Little Emily. In late 20th-century reality, it is a great port city, busy, bustling, full of traffic. Finding The Anna Sewell Tea Shoppe posed problems we did not encounter in the smaller towns.

A12, in East Anglia's dual carriageway system (interstate), became a fix for us in our more lengthy excursions, much as latitude and longitude for Columbus. In trips through and between smaller towns, we devised a short battle hymn for our confrontations with the ubiquitous roundabouts, or traffic circles: "In and out, Tooth and snout, We survive the roundabout!" Snug in The Keep, with maps fluttering like banners, we were off to A12 to conquer Yarmouth. Lowestoft's bustle and congestion gave a taste of what awaited in Great Yarmouth, but the Anna Sewell Tea Shoppe on Church Plain was waiting. Thinking of David Copperfield's message for Peggotty ("Barkis is willin'!"), we exuded the same confidence and continued on.

We had our usual snafus with town centre and the information centre. Signs sent us on until we were near the area, then mysteriously disappeared. After four attempts at getting directions, GSL, Navigator-Archivist, hit on a brilliant scheme. I asked a taxi driver how to get to the information centre. He was exactly right and specific with his instructions. But the centre was closed! Some thoughtful person did advise us, though, in a note stuck to the door, "Make inqueries at 1 South Quay." A problem of textual intention and, subsequently, textual interpretation, arose. Yarmouth has a North Sea waterfront and the Bure River waterfront. We were on the North Sea at town centre. South Quay was across town centre. So we reasoned we needed to go to the river. At the river, signs sent us back to the sea. As we passed town centre the third time, GSL/Navigator-Archivist, pleaded, "Now where is that Sea Front sign?"

Sergeant-Major/Vicar's-Wife replied with the equanimity of soul created by years of soothing agitated church members, "Down by the water."

But then, on one of our innumerable trips on the roundabout, I saw . . . A TAXI DRIVER. And being a creative Navigator/Archivist, I cut through all of life's stress and hopped out to ask about Anna Sewell's Tea Shoppe. We were close—half a mile from The Priory and Parish Church of St. Nicholas, which I could see, but we had to "go all the way to the left to double back at the top of the road on a roundabout . . ."

It was worth the effort!

On a lane of buildings, many of them antique shops now, just outside the church wall, was the Tudor house, three rooms stacked on top of each other, maybe two deep (at least the first floor ran three back) with diamond leaded glass windows and a wonderful pole lamp in front. The wall was painted white, except for the brick one to the right as we entered, as were the beams painted, but in dark brown. Its floor of large gray "stone" tiles seeped antiquity, affirming 1641 above the front entry door with the big ring handle. Trestle tables and chairs and benches were light brown. Squares of dainty place mats had pink and yellow flowers on cream background, colors repeated in large, soft paper napkins, folded to points and splayed from a glass container in table centers. A small brown-red goblet-shaped holder of a dried arrangement sat beside the napkins.

The fireplace covered half, well, a third of the room's width. Beneath an enormous bent beam mantel with black painted brick breast work, a fire danced on a grate. Above the mantel was a framed christening dress. Another one decorated the wall behind it in the next tiny dining area. Wall sconces with double lights were placed in strategic places. Between them hung color illustrations, framed, from *Black Beauty*, Anna's book. We later discovered the book that had been sacrificed for the pictures. It was lying on the table by the wall, for sale, for 80 pence ($1.25) with a few other things: a smaller book for 40 pence (.63 cents) and small packaged pot pourri. I guess if tearing up a book can be justified, it would be in this case.

The menu duly noted the place as "Anna Sewell Tea Shoppe, The Birthplace of the Authoress of Black Beauty" with its picture, and address, on the front. On the inside cover was a wonderful presentation:

> "Since their earliest introduction to high society, the unique qualities of fine teas have become universally

appreciated and the tradition of tea drinking has woven itself into the very fabric of the British way of life.

"Tea is an essential ingredient of those daily interludes, quiet and relaxation, sought by all during the turmoil of modern life, which have become enshrined in the ubiquitous tea-break, be it the morning 'cuppa' or a Palm Court tete-a-tete.

"Here at Anna Sewell Tea Shoppe we aim to maintain this great British ritual by serving some of the world's finest teas, prepared to perfection and attractively presented in this beautiful historic building.

"So relax for a while with a reviving cup of tea; try some of our delicious food and savour the tranquil atmosphere of these delightful surroundings."

The three combinations were:

*Anna Sewell Tea*
    Pot of tea of choice (I had Assam)
    Toasted crumpets (like "English muffin") with Butter and Jam
    Cake — chocolate

*Afternoon Tea*
    Pot of tea of choice (SM-VW had Breakfast Tea)
    Toasted tea cake (like a slightly sweet hamburger bun with currants)
    Cake — lemon

*Royal Tea*
    Pot of tea of choice
    Salmon and cucumber sandwiches
    Scone with jam and fresh cream
    Selection of cake

*Cream Tea*
> Pot of tea of choice
> Scone with Jam and fresh cream

Our waitress was the proprietor, Mrs. Peek, a young, bright, perky charmer with a broad smile and her blond hair piled on top of her head. At first, I said she was "thirty-ish," and SM-VW said 14. Later, we both decided 10, from the state of her skin and complexion. Cheery, business-like, she wore a beautiful light blue shirt with black skirt and black heels. In talking with her, we learned the house had been an antique shop before it gained its present function. She and her husband had bought it a year earlier, renovated it, and opened a tea shop. We heard her husband's voice in the kitchen. The two did all the work. While the shop was open, he took the kitchen and she doubled as hostess and server. Tea was presented in white ironstone, in octagonal shape, with square handles on the cups.

Anna Sewell's life story, such a sad one, was sketched on the back of the menu. Although 38 million copies of the book, now considered a classic, have been sold, and movies have insured its permanence in visual culture, Anna and her family were paid twenty English pounds for it, all the money they ever received of its earnings. The account reminds me again of how an artist's creativity is seldom a return to the person beyond the creative act. Others thrive, though, and maintain themselves on the work in many ways, a system that seems grossly UNFAIR!

We left in five o'clock traffic from Great Yarmouth heading to Norwich, marveling at ourselves—in a foreign country, no one in the world knowing where we were, in heavy traffic, and not an idea where we would spend the night because we had not yet secured a B&B. We congratulated ourselves on marrying men who did not worry about us, or think we were crazy, and even seemed agreeable to staying married to us. There was a sense of coming home as we met the Norfolk sign upon re-entry from Suffolk. Though just five days since we'd started, it seemed ages since we'd been in Diss, the place where we stayed our first night out from London. We felt that we, like the buildings, should wear a date somewhere. And London! Well, I could scarcely remember it. That was seven days ago. The encounter with the substance, or loaf, of Anna Sewell's tragic youth is balanced, at least now, by her lovely book and the exquisite tea room her home now houses which pays tribute to her talent. Far more remains to mark her passing than that which endures for Clary Smith whose tombstone we passed in the St. Nicholas churchyard, "hard by" the Anna Sewell house. Three lines announced simply: Clary Smith, died 16 June 1808, aged 12. His smaller text proclaims another childhood tragedy. With this book's bread-making capacity to create loaves of essence, I will add Clary Smith as a hyacinth to the lovely bloom which stands as The Anna Sewell Tea Shop. The complex tincture reminds that guarantees for fame and durability neither enlarge from power nor constrict because of fragility.

## ⊸⟾ *Norich* ⟾⊸
## *Maid's Head Hotel*

Getting into Norwich and the "multi-storied car park" presented no small chore. One man I stopped said he was going to the car park and would direct us to it. Our goal was the Maid's Head Hotel where, our information assured us, charming teas were served.

With some asking and doubling back, we found the Maid's Head Hotel, a fine old 13th-century hotel with traditional service, on

Wensum and Palace Streets near the Cathedral. Our trek up the crown of one of Norich's hills where the hotel stands was a cartoon-like zig-zag sketched by the stops and starts for directions. A man in a pub came out to direct us the final way. To my surprise, a monument to Edith Cavell, a nurse executed by the Germans as a spy in World War I, stands in front of the hotel. My earliest foray into education resulted in a nursing degree. I have always remembered Edith Cavell from my nursing history class because of her dramatic life. Born in 1865, the daughter of the Rector at Swardeston, she grew up strictly Victorian, but asserted her independence by becoming a nurse and finishing her preparation when she 22. With a successful career of almost 20 years as her qualifications, at 41, she became a matron at a clinic in Belgium. When the Germans invaded in 1914, she was com-pelled to remain. Arrested in August of 1915, she was executed Octo-ber 12, 1915, on orders of the German High Command, for aiding Allied soldiers to escape to Holland. Before her death, she said to the English Chaplain in Brussels, "I know that patriotism is not enough. I must have no hatred or bitterness toward anyone." Accorded a near royal funeral in Westminster, she is buried at Norwich Cathedral and her statue recalls her heroism for those who pass.

The Maid's Head Hotel on Tombland is famous. Half East Anglian, Queen Elizabeth I slept there in 1578. Her mother's family, the Boleyns, came from Blickling nearby. Her grandfather, Sir William Boleyn, is buried in the Cathedral. Sir John Paston men-tioned it in one of the Paston Letters in 1472. Because we arrived early, we took morning coffee in the lounge of the Maid's Head amidst muted colors and old elegance, off a tiny garden which was almost an atrium, and apparently a meeting place to transact busi-ness as well as pleasure. I saw and heard an earnest 40-ish woman talking "English-ly" to a man: ". . . and I just call my agent . . . that's

what agents are for, don't you think? . . . I just sign where he marks
. . . the whole thing befuddles me . . ." Two men discussed redecora-
tion as they walked around making notes, and slowly went up the
stairs continuing their jottings: " . . . and right there was where
someone cut around a closet . . ."

We resumed our own business at the Maid's Head. The china
was Royal Doulton Hotelware, brown and white, decorated with a
maid's head in brown which repeated the browns, tans, and creams,
in the room which contributed to the quiet atmosphere of the room.
Perusing the tea information, we noted on the menu:

> Traditional English teas are served 3:30 — 5:30
> Teas: cakes, pastries, gateaux, pies
> Cream teas: 2 scones, strawberry preserves, cream
> Full Afternoon Tea: Cakes, Sandwiches, brown bread/
> butter/ preserve

Exiting the Maid's Head, but intending to return, we set out to
explore other tea possibilities not included in our basic information.
We took pictures at the Edith Cavell monument and patronized the
Information Centre, adjacent to St. George Church on historic Elm
Hill, since we'd come across one that was open!

We chanced onto Elm Hill and Princes Street to Gedge of Elm
Hill, a patisserie that does teas. With its wares in the window and
wrought-iron and red inside, it is very picturesque. Gedge, a family
business about seven years old, operated a cake shop as well farther
up the hill toward The Mustard Shop, an advertising and promo-
tional scheme by the Colman company that has had phenomenal
success, so it has continued as a regular museum of mustard.

But those shops gave way to the cleverness of Jack Spratt's.

## ⋗═◦ *Norich* ◦═⋖
## *Jack Spratt's*

For sheer novelty in tea shops, we had to give our vote to Jack Spratt's. In the search for another hotel shop, we passed an American guitarist playing for donations. As mothers of sons his age, and with the thought that he might be working across Europe, we made a contribution. After other explorations around the area known as Castle Rock, we retraced to try to find a shop we'd seen earlier, passing, as we did, through the vari-colored tent-tops of the open market, which is how we found and settled in Jack Spratt's, a Dietary Tea Shop. The nursery rhyme was painted on the back wall, creating the cleverness of the place with the help of a predominant red and white motif. The tablecloth's floral pattern with a bright blue and white overlay of oilcloth and red and white table decor substituted for the understatement of miscellaneous antiques which usually greeted us in the shops. White and red salt and pepper shakers sat in their own little dish; a metal tip pouring spout graced the pitcher which stood on white tables surrounded by white metal "bentwood" chairs. Cafe style curtains were of red and white large checks. Of course, the service came in red and white, Johnson Brothers Simplicity red and white stoneware, with white handled flat ware. But the foods were available at a serving table with a skirt of the same fabric and material as the cafe curtains, and tea came with salads, rather than cakes, cream, currants, and calories. We didn't need the server's verification that the shop was new.

With time flying, we set off for the direction of Bury St. Edmunds and whatever we could encounter along the way. Because we were facing a Bank Holiday weekend, the need to secure housing was essential. With the loaf of Edith Cavell's example on the same

Kett's Tea Shop — North Walsham

day we encountered a young fellow ex-patriate, we drew the robe of
shared British example about us in the hyacinth of the Maid's
Head's charm and Jack Spratt's whimsy.

## North Walsham
## Kett's

With the usual map-squinting, sign-checking, and direction-
asking, we made it to North Walsham. While we were trying to find
one shop, which did not work out, we found Kett's, which did.
Tudor, built in 1580, it had a delightful room next to the one where
we were served, its half floor raised about eight inches, making the
low ceiling lower, to create a room which appeared to be a special
haven for short people. Tudor pictures hung on the white walls of
the beamed interior, alternating with armor and copper items,
especially near the windows. Large terra cotta squares made the
floor. In the window opposite me, at one end of the room, stood a
brass samovar. At the other end, a window hosted a copper kettle.
Above each window, a big long-handled copper pot was suspended
near two lights wired into the window beam. A bentwood hall tree
stood nearby with a fuzzy brown sweater hanging on it. A long-
handled 'slice,' the square utensil used to pull bread from brick
ovens, was secured to the wall behind me. The fireplace in the room
where we sat had a massive beam for a mantel, and in it were big
bellows and cooking utensils. My working eyes continued to survey
surroundings as we ate from Johnson willow stoneware delicious
breads, called cheese rolls, which seemed more like hamburger buns
full of grated cheese. Desserts came in compotes. Kett's was an
exquisite find.

*The Cockerel Tea Room*

## ⋯⋙ *North Walsham* ⋘⋯
## *The Cockerel*

On our way to The Cockerel, across the market area and down the hill, I stopped to examine a huge pavilion in the middle of the street. A sign educated and instructed me about the structure, the North Walsham Market Cross:

1549 — Built by Bishop Thirlby

1600 — Damaged by fire. Repaired by Bishop Redman.

1897 — Thoroughly restored as a permanent memorial of Queen Victoria's Diamond Jubilee.

1914 — Conveyed to the town by the ecclesiastical commissioners.

1930 — Included by the commissioners of works in the list of ancient monuments of national importance.

A drinking fountain in elaborate stonework, a coronation commemoration of King George V and Queen Mary, maintains a sentinel in front of the entire arrangement.

The Cockerel continued the 19th- and early 20th-century ambiance we encountered from time to time. With a garden in front, the shop seemed somewhat like a cottage. An extremely loud bell rang in the foyer to announce entry into the white-painted building. A second door opened onto the dining room. Inside, the effect was cozy Victorian: dark, beamed roof, pink and yellow rose print on black on the ceiling repeated the same pattern in the drapes. Priscillas at the window glass and a bed warmer hanging on the cream-colored, streak-textured walls emphasized the period. Swing music from the 1930s-40s was playing. A canary in a cage by the cash register sang with it: "Somebody loves me . . ." I tapped my foot and stared about. Black-painted wide boards, with the paint peeling in places, provided a floor. A wine rack on the wall served as coat rack. Four sets of four lamps with red fringed shades in the ceiling, and repeated as sconces between the windows, supplied the lighting.

" . . . You belong to my heart . . ." My mind hummed the notes. A beamed brick chimney framed a huge Russian Blue cat asleep in a chair by the fireplace, giving the appearance of a big fat basketball preventing anyone's sitting in the chair. He woke and came over to chat with me. Cats do that because they instantly recognize cat-people. Cats and cat-people are privy to a common language. Like the British birds in their articulation, he purred with an accent.

"Amour . . . Amour . . ." My mind hummed along. Landscape prints occupied the wall spaces. The picture nearest us was a Victorian embroidered scene of children by a pond, boys in sailor suits, girls in hats and pinafores, feeding a goose and goslings. Just beyond, a black-painted bookcase with cream-colored interior in five sections, three-fourths the length of the wall, showcased blue and white dishes.

"It had to be you . . ." I launched into another silent sing-along.

The shop had nine tables, in mixed style, and chairs with red cushions. In chatting with us, the proprietor shared the building's history. Two hundred years old, it once was a pub, but has been a tea room the past seven years. A poem over the fireplace caught my attention. I read it, and then copied it while the strains of . . . "How much do I love you? . . ." made my pen a metronome.

> The Cockerel is a tea room
> North Walsham is where it is
> It's run by Ann and Peter Downs
> With friendliness and fizz.
> A public house it used to be

Called The Cockerel
With painted doors and painted walls
It really looks quite swell.

A bird hangs from the ceiling
Singing its twittering song
I'm sure it gets quite tired,
Singing all day long.
A grandad clock in the corner
Ticks away the hours
The tables are all spruce and clean
And all decked out with flowers.

A sketch of a rooster decorated the bottom of the page, a fowl standing as proud as Chaucer's Chanticleer, to proclaim the courage engendered by confidence. Our North Walsham loaf rises from the sturdy endurance of history that can be spanned in the mind or crossed in a walk from Kett's to The Cockerel to recall to mind that tea and the quiet pleasure of congeniality can bloom like a hyacinth in unexpected places.

## ⊷⟾ *Wroxham Barns* ⟾⊶
## *Old Barn Tea Room*

In spite of the hovering spirits of The Killer Ss (Sidney, Spenser, and Shakespeare), on occasion the power of our Southwestern USA, Oklahoma-style culture nudged aside the grandeur of Britain. At those times, as we re-entered The Keep, we would belt out a phrase or two in honor of Willie Nelson: "On the road again." In that spirit of roaming the countryside, we found Wroxham Barns. The Old Barn Tea Room is in a restored archaic barn which houses an arts and crafts center like one we visited in Snape Maltings near Ipswich. Exuding comfort and a pastoral essence, it charmed with its rusticity. The picnic tables, self-service, and the tranquillity of the setting created a feeling of naturalness that could almost be touched. And the birds! British birds are incredibly vocal. They sound as though they have to be heard above Parliament's chitterings when a Prime Minister speaks. In city, town, or countryside, British birds announce themselves unabashedly. Chucked full with bravado and unbelievably determined to be heard, they carry on their communications. They seem not so concerned with being seen—they are just vociferous, clamoring above other sounds.

We were so mesmerized by the Old Barn and the different approach to tea that we did not pursue the more traditional rooms we had targeted in Wroxham and nearby Coltishall. In the Broads, where water transports and animals meander together, we were content to nibble the loaf provided by agriculture in an agrarian setting enhanced by the dandelion-like hyacinths of regional crafts viewed from a barn's picnic tea table.

## ⊷ *Horsham St. Faith* ⊷ *Elm Farm Chalet Hotel*

Toward Norwich, the Elm Farm Chalet Hotel at Horsham St. Faith provided another rustic setting for tea. We "took tea" in a pleasant old house which contains the lounge and dining room primarily. Newer buildings for the hotel and apartment units clustered about the gardens and gravel court entry. We were served in the dining room with a view of colorful, tranquil English gardens, giving an impression of red and white, brick and plaster in green on green.

Contrary to most of our findings, the tea room's look was contemporary: oak parquet floors, gold-colored glass lamps, white walls, brown and beige drapes, and light furniture, with tweeds and autumn colors in the prints of seat cushions which communicated a Danish modern kind of feeling. Jonquils in a vase matched the green and white Wedgewood metallic bone china. Place mats repeated the pastoral scenes. A hanging plant created a transition for a brick-lined arched doorway leading from the room to the entry hall and the gardens beyond. Loaf? The English countryside. Hyacinth? Tea taken in tranquility.

*Angel Hotel — Bury St. Edmunds*

# IV.
# Loaves and Hyacinths in Abbey Towns
⇢═ *Bury St. Edmunds* ═⇠
*Angel Hotel*

Abbey towns held special significance during England's medieval period. That importance continued well into the modern era because of the economic activities, intellectual environment, spiritual significance, and social interaction which developed about those places where the monasteries and convents located. Bury St. Edmunds was one of the most influential of the many abbey towns.

We intended to make Bury St. Edmunds our first Bed-and-Breakfast stop on the trip up from London. The shock of not getting lost in the departure from London meant we made it to the freeway, or dual carriageway as the British term such a highway, in fine style, full of confidence, and headed toward Cambridge on the M 11. Originally, we planned to turn off at Great Chesterford and wind our way northeast. However, the London luck left us, we missed turns, and continued on to the Cambridge exit. We had a brief view of the fabled place as we traveled through Newmarket on our way to Bury St. Edmunds. I cannot recall seeing anything quite so exquisite as watching Cambridge appear through the car windows gradually from the distance, then forge closer to recede in the distance. Since we were returning later, we let the visual delight sustain us. Cambridge was just as I had imagined, only better: a rare experience. Usually imagined places, experienced only through written texts, disappoint, but not Cambridge. New to our quest, we judged Bury St. Edmunds a bit too industrial for our purposes, so we decided to search around for a more atmospheric place where we might stay for several days.

A week later, after meandering in various directions and episodes, we returned to the area, just hours ahead of a Bank Holiday weekend when housing was not only a possible problem, but also a probable one. With time flying, we set off for the direction of Bury St. Edmunds and whatever we could encounter along the way. We headed south to Fornham St. Martin (following the directions to Brandon, a name we loved) and pulled into a post office two miles away from Bury St. Edmunds. Recalling our success with taxi drivers, we determined to utilize the knowledge of other public servants. We asked the storekeeper/postal clerk about a B&B since we preferred not going all the way into town if we didn't have to do so. At first he said he did not know of one, but then remembered he did have a business card of one in the area; however, he had locked himself out of his cubicle. He took a chair outside, climbed through a window into his place of business as postman, and came out smiling with the business card of the Fornham St. Genevieve and Broad Acre B&B, run by Norma and Norman Less. With his most impeccable British manners, the man explained how to find the establishment. Waving us on our way, he repeated, "Turn right at the trees where you came in, then hard left." Of course, we went three miles in all directions before we got to the Fornham St. Genevieve and Broad Acre B&B, run by Norma and Norman Less.

During our trek back and forth across East Anglia, I also functioned as the booking emissary; all archivists do that task sooner or later in the process of research. Our continuing problem lay in wanting two singles because we worked when we parted, and kept different hours. Single rooms, we learned, took care of the divergent flow of our labor patterns and rhythms. But that concept is probably too American where space and creative privacy are not national birthrights. Where lack of space is second nature, our request for two singles from two compatriot women traveling in a strange country raised more than several sets of eyebrows. But at the Less establishment, it was more.

I asked, "Do you have two singles?"

Norman Less responded, "For how long?"

"Three nights."

"We have doubles. And one single."

"I'll consult my friend." . . . Back. "Could we rent a double and a single?"

"Well, it's a holiday . . ."

"We realize that. We'll pay the double price."

"But it's just 9.50 a person."

Five rounds of attempting to explain we were happy to pay 19.00 to have a double and a single seemed futile. One person paying the charge for a double room was too foreign a concept.

"Let's see. We could give you singles tomorrow, perhaps. You see, it's a holiday."

"We understand. And we don't want you to lose money. If you'll let us have two rooms for three people, we'll pay whatever you'd charge three people."

Light! "Ah! I suppose we could do that." He consulted with his wife for the fourth time, then returned. "Yes. We'll give you the doubles tonight and move you tomorrow if necessary. We won't charge you extra unless we have to turn someone away." Ah, the fairness! The place was so well-situated, and comfortable, and our hosts so compatible, we stayed three nights and devoted three full days to the region. A lesson we learned, which seems almost parabolic, is that often the tea shop we were hoping to find did not function for our purpose, but in the process of looking, we found something else quite delightful that suited us better. We offer the Angel Hotel as evidence.

A grand old English establishment and a marvelous discovery, the Angel Hotel faces the ruins directly across from the Abbey remains at Bury St. Edmunds. It could serve as the film sets for a Victorian movie with its navy blue and rose decor, maroon velvet sofas, and padded arm chairs placed tastefully about the room with white-painted woodwork and papered in blue. "Candle" sconces and crystal chandeliers provided light. Ceramic figures on the mantel, two dogs and two people, guarded blue and white furniture groupings. They looked down on a hunt table, graced by a white bowl of flowers and ivy, with its half shape at the back of sofa across the room. They could not survey the pastoral painting above the mantel or the sconces to either side, as I could while I watched them watching the room. Framed caricatures of Victorian gentlemen, appearing very similar to those illustrations by Phiz, long-time collaborator with Dickens, surround the walls. Their top curved frames suit the brass and ceramic table lamps and the shelf effect at the top of the room with the ceiling with the curving up from it.

Our companions were no less interesting. A couple sat on the fireplace sofa, reading the paper; a woman alone was having coffee at our right. With newspapers available, we read the latest about the nuclear cloud in Chernobyl and terrorism endemic in our world. The hotel was quiet above the subtle hum of professional hotel keepers: turning newspaper pages; adding machine sounds; ringing clock chimes, more bell than chime; and greetings full of cheer, "Good morning. Another nice bright one. Your husband just collected the car keys."

We chanced upon information about John Appleby, an American airman from Arkansas, who had been in the region during WWII and written a book, *Suffolk Summer.* We looked for it in a shop window on the way out. With some surprise, we found it. Although the shop was closed, the reception manager brought the keys and took out two copies for us. Preliminary information told of a rose garden named for Appleby in the Abbey gardens and that proceeds from the book contributed to its upkeep. Both the reception manager and our tour book complimented Appleby's ability to capture East Anglia, being an American. We were amused—and decided if we were successful with our book, we'd buy a sign for the Appleby Rose Garden.

The Abbey is ancient and brooding. It is sobering to think our heritage of individual rights started right there with the barons meeting to determine to demand the Magna Charta from King John in 1214, which he signed the next year at Runnymeade. St. Edmund, killed by the Danes in 870, lived in the Abbey for a while. The Danes murdered him somewhere else, perhaps at Hoine. Legend teaches that a wolf helped the people find his body and head; hence the wolf appears on crests in the region. The town's origins fade into the misty veil of history. King Canute gave the Abbey its grant in 1032; it has a strong tie with Edward the Confessor. Throbbing back of the scrim of Anglo-Saxon legends exists the outline of a wavering, but very real, loaf outline that still contributes to present characteristics for modern descendants of Old English realities. The hyacinth experienced at the Angel Hotel reclaims a nineteenth-century atmosphere which US Airman John T. Appelby from Arkansas reflects and East Anglia validates by the rose garden which bears his name in the Abbey ruins. I feel drawn to John T. Appelby because he and my mother both hail from Arkansas. I grew up hearing the stories of Arkansas, so my senses reach out to the essence he left. I wish I could find him to tell him how the remnant of his sojourn pulses and touches my trek where he trod. I would like to tell him the earlier legends of the Danelaw and Alfred the Great and Hadrian's Wall and the Anglo-Saxon Chronicles. And I would ask him in exchange to teach me to do brass rubbings and show me the sites of his wartime visits which kept him sane and productive in the midst of madness. Loaves and hyacinths should be shared.

## ⤖ *Wymondham* ⤗
## *Sinclair Hotel*

Energized by the added dimensions of insight and awe contributed by Bury St. Edmunds, we were disposed to investigate other abbey towns as we found them so identified. At Wymondham (pronounced "Windam") we detoured into town because it looked good at the roundabout and one of our most reliable tour books rhapsodized about its unique Market Cross: a Tudor style edifice, with a round, peak roof, weathervane, open first floor, and enclosed top.

In Norma's vast readings on the British tea room, one source declared that the way to find the best tea shop in town was to follow the "little old ladies." Because we were responding to impulse, we decided to ask Wymondham's "little old ladies," since we seemed not to have taxi drivers or bobbies at hand. Eager advice sent us to the town's beautiful old hotel on "High," the Sinclair Hotel, 28 Market Street, where Paul and Josie Hawkins were proprietors. The model of graciousness, they took us to the lounge, a quiet room with salmon-tangerine velvet-covered chairs. Drapes of the same fabric and color hung at the windows which were further gowned with sheer glass curtains, ivy on the sills, and four brass wall lamps. Four round brown tables with chair legs displaying the table style announced they were matched sets. In the vase, we recognized a spray of carnations and other white flowers we didn't know as the omnipresent fresh flowers. Across the lounge, Greek figures with a mirror back of them posed a trans-cultural suggestion and made me think of John Keats's poem, "Ode to a Grecian Urn." The contemporary colors and the hint of classicism suggested by the figures contributed a curiously eclectic charm which the brown and white stoneware reinforced and the carpet, brown and white, in a laced bamboo effect, emphasized. From the serving bar, brick below the counter, our traditional cream tea was dispatched. At Wymondham's Sinclair Hotel, the ambiance and the tea experience almost submerged us in an Alice in Wonderland reversal to interchange the place as hyacinth and the event as the loaf.

*Ickworth Butler's Tea Shop*

# V.

# Loaves and Hyacinths in Great House Environs

*⟫ Horringer ⟪*
*Ickworth Butler's Tea Shop*

Continually, we amazed ourselves by where we would finish each day. The day we found Ickworth and the Butler's Tea Shop, we left Sudbury to go to Cavendish first, then planned to go to Aylsham to travel in the north of East Anglia. But we ended in the opposite direction.

The road to Cavendish goes through Long Melford, another of the wool villages, still in the Stour Valley. Its high (main) street is 2 1/2 miles long and demonstrates many architectural styles which house shop after shop, an antique searcher's heaven. When I stopped to buy a paper, we learned the Duchess of Windsor had died and that Scotland Yard was still at work on the London bombing. We knew not to tell at home that we passed that very corner on Oxford in front of Selfridges on the double decker the day before the bomb exploded. In the process of getting, or fetching, the paper, I asked for directions to Melford Hall, a great house just off the high street, and a Mrs. Adams's bakery which was supposed to be one of two faggott-fired bakeries of East Anglia. According to our sources, Mrs. Adams and her daughters ran the business, but I learned she no longer has it. However, I was told that The Cock and Bell had morning coffee and afternoon tea. We decided to check out Melford Hall, Kentwell Hall, and the Church of the Holy Trinity. Melford Hall has been in the Hyde-Parker family since the 18th century and now houses valuable furniture, old paintings, and Chinese porcelain. Some of the men in the family were sailors and brought home many interesting artefacts. We were too early for Melford, and Kentwell's tea room was not serving until a month later, when we would be gone. Moreover, the church was locked (yes, we were out early), but we looked around its environs.

We decided to go on to Cavendish, since we had a tea room there on our list, and check out B&Bs as we went, but had no success on either search. However Cavendish, another of those thatched, color-washed villages in the Stour, was delightful. Back at The Cock and Bell, we had coffee to reassess and revamp the day's travel plans. The exercise sent us to Bury St. Edmunds with the intention to attempt to remain centrally located for the weekend to finish scouting Essex, and save the north for later.

When we embarked on our fruitless search for a Bed-and-Breakfast at Bury St. Edmunds, we discovered there was no information center open, so we went to the police station after several sets of instructions on how to find it. My travel notebook is filled with funny maps and written directions. At the station, we met Florence Rose, an officer in the Constabulary, who gave us the names of three B&Bs and a new lead on a tea room. She told us of Mrs. Zoe Ward in Horringer, "hard by" Ickworth Mansion, the region's great house. According to what Florence told us, Mrs. Ward, who lived at Cedar Cottage in Horringer, had just published *Curtsey to a Lady* about the family in the great house. And, continued our engaging informant, a tea room functioned nearby. Our exposure to British charm and sensitivity in the interaction with Florence was repeated when we returned to the station later. As we stood in line to ask about another matter, we witnessed an interesting display of British manners. A couple stood in front of us, ready to advance to the window when the man engaged there finished. The woman said to her companion, "Come back." The man with her did not understand what she wanted him to do. More explicitly, she said, "Step away. It might be personal." The helpful British spirit was further demonstrated by the response we received at the places where Florence sent us to find lodging. We couldn't get in The Chantry Guest House on Sparhawk, nor the White Hart on South Gate Street, nor the Dunstan on Springfield Road. But, in each case, we received friendly advice. At Dunstan, we were recommended to York House, and Mrs. Reeve there, who, after telling us she could not accomodate us, recommended the Regency Hotel, saying we were not to be "put off" by a hotel, that it was nice, and she was getting "good reports."

The most productive result from that particular search came from the information about the Great House, Ickworth, the home of the Hervey family, which came into possession of the Manor of Ickworth in 1485 and joined the aristocracy when a Hervey was made Earl of Bristol in 1714. The family seemed to have a knack for surviving difficulties with fortunes expanded by weathering political and religious storms and marrying well. Stature increased when the 5th Earl was created Marquess. We started south to look for it near Horringer, and to find Mrs. Zoe Ward to buy her book, *Curtsey to a Lady*, about life around Ickworth. By the time we made that decision, we knew that she was born in Horringer, her father ran the post office, and she was head mistress of the school until she retired.

We found Ickworth, a massive Palladian structure, approached by a curving road through early morning "misty, moisty" sheep meadows. Expansive grounds surround it. A pink farmhouse on the estate grounds, across the way en route to the great house, cast color on the scene. Signs instructed us when Ickworth was open for viewing; we were too early in the season. We drove through town twice, saw a large tea shop, and stopped a paper boy for directions to Cedar Cottage, Mrs. Ward's house. The paper boy, representing a new job category on our list of "guides" to consult, also said the tea shop was not open on weekends. Cedar Cottage was located right by the gate to Ickworth. I went to the door, and am sure I woke Mrs. Ward. With my best attempt at good manners, given the fact that I appeared at her door with the sun, I told her Florence Rose at Bury St. Edmunds Police Station told us about her book. With words trailing, I concluded, "My friend and I wondered where could we buy a copy."

After a few seconds of silence which covered whatever immediate response she might have preferred to make, she said with politeness, "Well—of course—the book shop in Bury—but, also, at the post office across the street."

Since I was standing knee-deep in my quagmire of presumption, I forged on. "Would you be willing to autograph a copy for us?"

"Yes, of course."

Jubilant, and with many apologies for my forwardness, I dismissed myself from her door. In The Keep, we returned to the town centre and the post office where a problem awaited us; the post office didn't open until 9 a.m. But time was never wasted. We had a series of quests when we had time loops in our searches. One was to make quick detours to find country churches. For half an hour, we drove in the country, looking for a church in the mists. We found it at Chedburgh, down a road guarded by trimmed hedgerows, which, with every glimpse through them, made me think of how England was changed by land enclosure. On a slight rise, the church sat placidly by the most fascinating cluster of tombstones. Each was topped with a very simple

Celtic cross, so they looked like heads from a distance. And with their leaning every way, they appeared as twittering old friends, looking down at a couple who had fallen on the ground. The "fallen ones" were two sarcophagi, one belonging to Thomas Abraham Rawlinson, Esquire, Barrister-at-Law, who died 11 July 1859, and his wife, Emma, who died in 1855. The hovering group were too old to have legible engraving on them. Thomas was the elder brother of the parish rector. With our usual fantasies over possible narratives for the permanent inhabitants in the churchyards, our extra time passed quickly.

We scurried back to Horringer to the post office to get the book, deciding to check at the tea shop as we went by to see if we could come for tea anyway. Not only were they not closed, they were a FIND. Run by Mr. and Mrs. Lee, Mr. Lee was butler to the 4th Marquess at Ickworth for 27 years, and stayed with the same family 34 years. His house, the tea room, is the butler's house. He and his wife turned it into a tea room when Mr. Lee retired from service at Ickworth. Mrs. Lee came from the kitchen to greet me; she was baking in preparation for the day. With cheery exuberance, she told me they could seat 45 and launched into a description of their lovely antiques used everyday in service. She showed me one Victorian tea table in particular.

"It can be used for cards, you see," she said, as she folded parts of table leaves up and down. I observed, charmed by the room with its creme, gray, and beige striped wallpaper and pink ceiling. Another of the unusual tables was one octagonal shaped with a tray underneath. While we chatted, I looked at the table ware, Polka Dot by Alfred Meakin, the exact complement for the aqua carpet and floral drapes with white Priscillas at the glass. Mr. Lee came out, introduced himself, and told me the menu.

"Today we are serving brown bread and butter, scones, cake, jam, and a pot of tea. One pound fifty." They weren't open yet, but

*Time for Tea*

he invited me to return. After I promised him we would try to get back, Mr. Lee added that they also had hand-painted trivets (by a friend) for sale. I assured him we would love to look at them.

The Keep retraced the way to the post office and the book. We took our copies to Cedar Cottage, across the street. Mrs. Ward invited us in while she autographed them, and our mission was complete. We went back to Horringer for SM-VW to see Mr. and Mrs. Lee and to experience their service. While we took our tea, we sat by a small window; a one panel priscilla tie-back allowed the sun to spill onto a tiny pot of flowers. Mr. and Mrs. Lee were very chatty. She said, "My hubby was the butler at Ickworth. I used to go up to see all the silver out when he worked on it. Oh, it was lovely. And the gold. Pity we don't have that any more."

He told of going into service as a footman, being in the war, and returning to become the Earl's butler eventually. I asked him about a taped interview, to which he agreed, but at the point of beginning, he was called to the back by a neighbor who was going to Holland and wanted to give instructions about the care of his things. Mrs. Lee came after a while to say to us she was afraid we'd need to come back, because her "hubby" could not leave at the moment. We could not, of course, and I was quite disappointed because of the informational treasure Mr. Lee appeared to be. When we were in the car and about to leave, Mrs. Lee came to the door and called after us, "You gave me too much!" She was referring to the tip.

Both Mrs. Lee and Mrs. Ward echoed in their comments each other's longing for the stability of the old ways, and the Lees, providers of service and contentment of satisfaction in that service, rendered, with the honor of the work as its own reward, the kneading for a loaf worthy of guarding. The Butler's Tea Room houses the fading flower of that hyacinth which only enhances its value and fragrance.

# ⊷ *Blickling near Aylsham* ⊷
# *Blickling Hall Tea Room*

We targeted Aylsham, a place of Dutch gables and wherries up the River Bure, as one of our hubs, a place where we might stay several nights, as we explored during the days. Known in the Middle Ages for its production of worsted cloth and linen, the town has endured for ages in the Broads, the estuary system. Listed in Domesday with Danish domination, the area later went to John of Gaunt, who founded its church in 1380. Fanny Burney, King's Lynn authoress of *Evelina* and other popular novels, visited her sister Charlotte who lived in Aylsham with her surgeon husband in the 1790s.

Two miles from the village sprawls Blickling palace and estates, first belonging to King Harold, or Harald, in its old spelling, last of the true English kings and a true East Anglian. It passed hands several times—once to Sir John Fastolf (Shakespeare modeled Falstaff on him), and then to Geoffrey Boleyn who went on to London (as did Dick Whittington) to become Lord Mayor. Three generations of Boleyns lived there until Anne's execution by Henry VIII. The history of the owners before and since comprises a complicated list of climbers ascending the ladder rungs into various levels of the aristocracy through exploited opportunity, political favor, and, of course, prestigious marriages.

The B&B we had listed for Aylsham did not have a couple of singles. We were sent out to Spa Farm, and we wondered why we agreed to go, as we crept along a dirt road with high dirt lawn covered "walls" to an opening. Then a wonderful vista spread before us—a working farm, replete with a huge brick barn, rolling meadows, a beet farm, and a magnificent old two story brick farmhouse. Mrs. Gosling, the lady of the house, told us later that parts of it were 300 years old. In fact, one section was considered Tudor, but the wall was covered with plaster and we could not examine the architecture. It had been two houses during the war, but was converted to one again afterward. We met the family's teenage daughter, Marie. Mr. Gosling was out plowing the field. When he rode in on the tractor, the British love for dogs was exhibited once more. A big dog sat up beside him like another person, and obviously had been there all day.

Upon our arrival, our hostess served us tea in a living room graced by old photographs of the farm sixty years ago. She and her family have had it 22 years. A piano with movable candle sconces mounted on its front added its own sense of stability. We looked at photographs of harvest scenes taken from the front, with a view of the house as it had appeared architecturally several decades ago. We fell in love with Spa Farm and stayed three nights, venturing forth during the day with ease because of its proximity to a highway.

As impressive as the working farm was in its antiquity, even more notable to me was its placid continuity in the neighborhood of historic Blickling, just two miles from where we slept each night. Seymour, author of one of our guide books, is right. You think you've made a wrong turn when Blickling appears suddenly: first the church, then the buildings, lawns, and great house. Pinnacles and gables and red brick and prickly feelings of awe overwhelm the visitor!

The tea room is in the right building wing, facing the main hall, in the portion once used for stables, groomsmen, outdoor servants, and visiting servants. With high ceilings, beams in lighter wood, big square floor tiles of russet and cream terra cotta, it does not seem as ancient as the view across the sweeping lawns, past the moat garden, to the great house facade. Painted salmon, the color is repeated in flowers on an oil cloth print on the tables that have a rustic look with their T-shaped leg bars. Chairs in the light wood have a contemporary look of office chairs. The ever present fresh flowers were about eight inches across, in a basket. The service counter held the usual tea offerings. We took ONE "Norfolk cream tea," (two scones, cream, butter and jam, and two cups of tea).

As we munched, we studied the surroundings. On the wall were photos of interiors at Blickling. A hutch at the room's end held an enormous copper pitcher. I think it would be hard to lift as it stood empty, and impossible, if anything were in it. In my fancy, I imagined the rise and fall of Anne Boleyn and her people. I thought of the setting with some ancestral patriarch striding across the gardens. I tried to picture Henry VIII and Anne together in some domestic scene, though they were never here. The sadness of the ill-fated daughter of this great house touched me greatly. And yet, how ironic that her daughter, Elizabeth, became the political reality for the son Henry transformed a kingdom to obtain. In the absence of that son, Anne's daughter out-Henried Henry to make Britain's great age her adjective: Elizabethan.

Although we came for tea, we decided to tour the house, an activity in which we rarely indulged because of our purpose being work. With the scare for tourist safety and being there early in the season, we practically had the place to ourselves. So we bought a guide book and sauntered through it: such a pleasure to wander along unhurried. The Jacobean ceilings and the library, especially the huge scale of the architecture, singularly impressed me. With the time out for tourism finished, we retraced our path to Spa Farm and Mrs. Gosling to think through our agenda for the rest of the week, then went to our rooms to work. But just outside Aylsham, we became involved in a traffic jam and witnessed an unforgettable sight at the same time. All travel stopped for a herdsman to cross the highway with his large drove of black and white cows.

When we left Spa Farm after three days, we headed north toward Cromer, in spite of the fact that Mrs. Gosling thought we should have gone into Norwich to see the Queen who was attending a stationer's fortieth anniversary that day. She sent us off with her fine sense of humor: "You are not going to see the Queen? Oh, she'll be so disappointed!"

Birds sing early and late in England. They seem as sociable as the ducks and dogs. The early morning jets reminded me of how vulnerable this land is, and always has been. Being there made me more appreciative of the European reluctance to jump at every supportive measure for American interests. Their risks are more immediate. At breakfast of the second day at Spa Farm, our hostess told us a Russian nuclear reactor blew up and that a radioactive cloud was drifting toward Finland and the Scandanavian area. Later, when we bought a paper, read Chernobyl for the first time, and heard the bad news during the day, I sensed the vulnerability that Europeans have faced and shrugged off through the centuries. I remembered Mrs. Gosling's question-answer when I asked if she was worried about the nuclear dust on Britain. "Will worry protect us?"

Will worry protect us? The thought becomes a sustenance loaf to ponder. When Anne Boleyn's family, two miles from Spa Farm, learned their most famous daughter had been executed, they had to know their survival was at stake, given the Court politics of Henry VIII. Perhaps Mrs. Gosling's question becomes a proverb for security in the atmosphere of Blickling where tea provides a hyacinth for the senses to ward off ominous feelings, whether they derive from the threats of an executioner's axe or a nuclear cloud.

*The Market Place — Framlingham*

# VI.
# Loaves and Hyacinths in
# Old Fort and Castle Towns

*Diss and Framlingham*
## *The White Hart*
## *The Market Place*

O
ur entry into the Framlingham region came with our first day
out from London. We intended to stay in the Bury St.
Edmunds area, but did not find a Bed-and-Breakfast readily. After a
great deal of driving, back-tracking, and exploring we found a
marvelous place farther north in Diss, with a lot of silliness and
punning that revolved around "Diss 'n Dat." Our shelter was an old
house with a Bed-and-Breakfast place around the corner from Scole
Inn, also known as The White Hart, which I think surely must be
the place that inspired Alfred, Lord Noyes to write "The Highwayman." The inn was built in 1655 by a wealthy Norwich wool merchant, John Peck, who commissioned the village carpenter, John
Fairchild, to build a large and richly furnished house suitable to
accommodate himself, fellow merchants, and all the "first families in
these counties." Charles II breakfasted there in 1671. Lord Nelson
was a guest. In its coaching inn days, a wide entrance led through
the front of the building where a bar now stands. Coaches could be
driven through the archway into the yard which is still flanked by
large stables. Little has been changed. The great stairway which

climbs both floors is considered one of the most important of its kind. John Belcher, the Highwayman, used the inn as his headquarters and regularly rode his horse up the massive staircase to hide it in one of the rooms when being hunted. Hoof marks can be seen in the stair tread. A gate was installed eventually at the stair's head to prevent such escapades, and remains in place.

One of the rooms is supposed to have a ghost of a woman, wrongly accused of infidelity by her husband. He brought her on a trip from Norwich and murdered her at the Inn. We did not investigate or attempt to verify the ghost sightings with research of our own.

The Sundial Room, which we did view, has a drawing on the wall dated 1706 depicting a huge circular bed which James Peck installed to offer separate beds for travelers arriving when the Inn was full. Thirty people could sleep, feet to the middle. The drawing, close to the window, was used by occupants to judge time as rays of the sun fell on it. Landlords through the years were instructed not to paint over it, and they have not.

We arrived too late for tea, so we waited to have dinner in the restaurant, a large room with a huge fireplace at either end. I could see holes in the sides of the one by me where spits had been. Our table for two had a formal setting with heavy silver, a silver bud vase with fresh daffodils, and a single heavy brass candle holder which was about two feet in height. I had the Table d'Hote dinner: wonderful bread, celery soup, chicken, four vegetables, raspberry souffle, and coffee. We could hardly walk out. Service for the entire room, which filled rather quickly, was done efficiently by two young women.

We were the only tourists among an all English clientele in the dining room, so Tudor in its appearance with heavy, dark woods, beamed ceilings and walls, and drapes and carpet in dark colors. We tried not to stare about at the wonderful study of faces, but my eyes kept returning to one man whose character played about the set of his jaw and the intensity in his eyes as he sat alone, eating a formal dinner, reading.

As I walked out and across the stones to the rooms, the gray clouds scudded across and about a full moon, reminding me again of that cobbled inn yard in "The Highwayman," and the words played in my memory: "The moon was a ghostly gallon tossed upon cloudy seas . . ." We turned to the street, saw the five gables of the roof in the night, and I walked in rhythm to the verses:

The road was a ribbon of moonlight over the purple moor,
And the highwayman came riding, riding,
The highwayman came riding, up to the old inn door.
Over the cobbles he clattered and clashed in the dark inn-yard.
He tapped with his whip on the shutters,
    But all was locked and barred.
He whistled a tune to the window, And who should be waiting there,
But the landlord's dark-eyed daughter, Bess, the landlord's daughter,
Plaiting a dark red love-knot into her long black hair.

To make it even more ethereal, a skeletal tree in our front yard at the B&B clutched the moon with claw fingered limbs.

The wind was a torrent of darkness among the gusty trees.
The moon was a ghostly galleon, tossed upon cloudy seas...

We went from Diss to Eye to Debenham, stopping to see moated farm mansion Crow Hall, en route to Framlingham, where Queen Mary, Elizabeth's half-sister, was hidden in the castle by sympathizing Catholics before she was crowned and gained fame as Bloody Mary. An exquisite serendipity was The Market Place in Framlingham,

*Tiffin's Tea Room*

just down the hill from the castle. A tea shop, the 350 years-old small stone house, stands independently, not sharing contiguous walls with other buildings, as the custom was. Built in 1640 as a residence, it has enjoyed varied uses through the years and opened as a tea shop in 1960. The proprietor, Andrew Hodson, served us. He was born in London, but his parents had a summer home in Aldeburgh, and he knew East Anglia well. Experienced in the restaurant business, young Mr. Hodson worked at Claridge's in London and was Deputy Manager at Simpsons-in-the-Strand. When he learned The Market Place was for sale, he bought it and brought a professional chef, Ian Chamberlain, from the Continent where he had gone for experience in Swiss and German hotels. In commenting on the continental air he has brought to Framlingham in The Market Place, Hodson said, "People have lived here all their lives without ever going to London." The Market Place serves all meals, but changes its pace with lovely, old-fashioned afternoon tea.

We trudged up the hill past the old church, finding a wonderful book store on the way as we tramped on to the castle. If those stones could talk! The massive moat runs down to a river that is both beautiful and eerie, in a way, with its whispers about the history it has witnessed. The ramparts above the moat, now dry and grassy, provide a glimpse into the size and extent of the old castle, and I stood very quietly to absorb any remaining emanations from the air of the scenes enacted on those walls. What if Mary had outlived Elizabeth? How would our culture and literature have played out? No golden age of Elizabeth? Would Mary have allowed Sidney, Spenser, and Shakespeare to survive? How would her Court have shaped what we are as Americans? Such heavy thoughts.

# ⤚⟶ *Framlingham* ⟵⤛
# *Tiffin's*

We tarried so long at The Market Place that we hastened on to make our schedule for the day, but returned to Framlingham three days later to visit Tiffin's Tea Room which we had "saved" from the first time we visited the town. Past narcissus fields and circular red brick houses with thatch roofs, we back-tracked to our road to discover Framlingham was hosting market day. After strolling through the spread wares, we detoured up a street to Tiffin's Tea Room where Patricia Macgregor, its proprietor, also made Tiffin's an antique shop. Half the fun of looking included the sprightly conversation with the shop's owner; Norma bought both a Victorian and an Edwardian tea tray cloth.

Tiffin's is tiny. Its delicacy matches the sense of Victorian miniatures in shadow boxes and doll houses. A lovely little blackboard scroll held a sign outside with "Tea" on it. Overflowing with antiques, dishes, candlesticks, pedestals, and dried flowers in a basket, the shop can seat ten. The dishes are "for trade, not sale to the public," Patricia Macgregor said. The information on the back was daunting. Two seals declared the ware's pedigree. One advised the commissioning was by appointment of Her Majesty, the Queen, to Manufacturers by ceramic tableware, and the other cited the Queen Mother's appointment also. The quantity of information and seals listed covered the backs of the plates:

> English Ironstone
> Stoke-on-Trent
> Pattern:  Hearts-on-Flowers
> Johnson Brothers

Stoke-on-Trent
England
Staffordshire
OLD GRANITE

An extra plate was almost needed to carry the information about the tableware.

While Norma shopped with Mrs. Macgregor, who told us of an antique fair in Dedham where she wanted to go, but her dog was "unwell" and anyway, she didn't have "transport," I watched people and sensed the life rhythm. When we walked through the market to return to The Keep, I found a fifty-year-old platter with blue border ("patent") like the Worcester Howard tea plates I bought in London. It cost one pound, 75 pence, or $2.77, on the pound/dollar exchange that particular week. I will cherish it.

Some curious sort of scale seems continually to balance thoughts and impressions between past and present, antiquity and modernity to mix loaves and hyacinths indiscriminately. The hurry and bustle of London, with the pleasure of the Jennings's (Norma's friends) London flat, see-saws with the receding years of The White Hart Inn and the moon on cobblestones. And the presence of "Bloody Mary" broods on Framlingham's old castle walls much as the inn's murdered wife in Diss keeps that woman's memory alive, while Patricia Macgregor at Tiffin's trades dishes commissioned by Queen Elizabeth II and Andrew Hobson brings the Continent to Framlingham in the person of his chef at The Market Place. A tea shop dreamer places loaves and hyacinths first on one side of the scale, and then on the other, as the gentle rocking indicates which should receive the weight.

*The Ship Stores — Clare*

## ·→══○ *Clare* ○══←·
## *Ship Stores Tea Room*

In our journey between Ipswich and Dedham, we discovered 3000 year-old Colchester, inhabited as early as the Bronze Age. Cunobelin (Shakespeare's Cymbeline) set up his capital there. Claudius took it in 44 A.D. and established Colonia Camulodunum, first Roman colony in Britain. The ancient Roman Castle on the spot was called Demesne. Boadicea, Queen of the Britons, tried to take it seventeen years later and drive out the Romans. After the Romans, came the Saxons who rebuilt it as Colneceaster. Danes repeatedly plundered it in the 9th and 10th centuries. In 1085, William the Conqueror built the castle which had Europe's largest keep at that time. His wall, 165 feet by 115 feet and 13 feet thick, lost its top story in 1683. That Norman castle, the present ruins, was built the second half of the eleventh century using the Roman materials. The Roman town wall, two miles in length and over 19 feet tall in places, still remains up to 10 feet high in places. But the tea shops in Colchester and along the coast, like the castle, were not open for our closer perusal the time we were there.

On we went to Castle Hedingham. Our same bad luck held; both shops we had listed for the area were unavailable; one was not open "for the season," and the other had closed permanently. Also, the castle was closed for usual tourist viewing. But we drove up the road as far as we could, and suddenly felt a castle hovering over us, scarcely visible through the fog! Hedingham, a massive Norman castle, was built by the Earls of Oxford around 1130. The keep, four stories tall, survives almost undamaged. It looms on a hill above the town. On a foggy, muted English day, the effect was intimidating. "Fog" is not quite sufficient as a word to depict the English variety of that phenomenon of weather which coats and transforms the physical aspects of life. In it, towns, castles, forests, and other evidence of reality assume and project a mystic dimension which only increase the willingness of one already disposed to do so to believe in the incredible.

We struck off for Clare and a tea shop called The Ship Stores to hit pay dirt! Clare is a gorgeous little village, the site of an Augustinian priory. Built in 1248, it was the birthplace of Lionel, Duke of Clarence, son of Edward III. Ancient houses in it date to the 15th century. The church of Saints Peter and Paul was constructed in the 14th and 15th centuries, though the West Tower is much older. Gothic font and 17th-century wooden furniture reinforce its aura of age. Mrs. Kies is the proprietor, cook, waitress, and hostess at The Ship Stores in a house built in the 1600s. Her husband tends the store in the next room to the one which houses her tea shop. She said the building was originally three houses that were joined at different times. Upstairs, a window shows the bricked-in spaces. Named "sheep stores" originally, the business became "ship" stores through usage because of the local phonetics—in her words, " . . . the lazy Essex way of saying sheep."

She and her husband were very busy during the time we had tea. The bell for the store rang repeatedly, and Mrs. Kies had five to seven in her ten-person capacity shop all the time we were there. Like a cottage, the shop was cozy and memorable. Dark colors on white dominate: white walls and ceiling, beamed dark wood. The furniture appeared ordered to specifications: three brown-black trestle tables for four that allow for room at the ends, ten chairs that are milking stools (reminding me of Tess from Thomas Hardy's novel) with key hole backs. The shop doubled for the Kies family's personal dining room when it was not open for service.

Windows were paned, not leaded, with frames painted white. Black and brown print curtains slid on a wooden bar by means of brass rings in the fabric. The Colclaugh china with its green, blue, and black leaf designs on white boasted a gold ring around the pieces. Tables were set with cork place mats, larger center mats for tea service, and smaller ones for a tiny round brown bowl with flowers at the upper table corner. While we waited for our order, I catalogued the room. A side board that alternated as a buffet had two doors, two drawers, and two open shelves. The shelves held a wicker basket of pink flowers, three blue and white plates, and other colors and shapes of dishes with three sets of brass salt and peppers, books and leaflets, and on top, three brasses.

The odd shaped chimney, part brick with a slope and the other half white plaster, was covered by an iron grate which held flowers and an electric pour-over coffee pot. The hand-written set tea bill of fare on a black board hung on the white part of the chimney. Two scones with tea and strawberry jam cost 75 pence ($1.18); an additional scone with butter, 45 pence (.71); tea cake, 35 pence (.55). A tall pedestal table by the door to the kitchen held two brass electric tea kettles. The black tea service on the table complemented the dark wood and wrought iron two-light sconces on the wall. Between them was hung an engraved village scene in a green matted silver trim frame.

As she served us, we chatted with Mrs. Kies, remarking on the huge church for a village the size of Clare. She explained that the enormous churches occurred as a result of competition between villages in previous centuries to show which was the wealthiest. Clare, she said, was granted a charter for market, which made it a town instead of a village, but it is really a village by size, she admitted. Our chatting ceased when a family, a mother, father, and little boy, came in.

The father appeared considerably older than the mother. They sat at the window. As before, I enjoyed watching the British interaction with children. The father and child discussed the buttons on the child's coat. Then the father told the boy where he had to sit during tea.

"Why this way?"

The answer was spoken with firm kindness, "Because you don't do as I tell you."

After a bit, the boy turned to smile at us, and began peeking at us through his chair back hole.

We finished our tea and left by way of Cavendish, checking The Olde School Room we missed earlier, and stopping across the street at Cavendish Antiques with 1751 in the plaster over the lintel. I bought three small volumes of Shakespeare, dated Leipzig, 1843, as a gift for my sister.

We turned homeward via Long Melford where we encountered an unbelievable traffic jam because of a Book Fair! In our detouring to avoid traffic like that we would expect on the way to a football game in our country, we visited a tea room in Kentwell Hall, a private residence and ancient manor house, which the new owners were planning to renovate and reclaim. Since we were in the area of a Great House, Melford Hall, we drove down the road a quarter of a mile to see that beautiful trust house. In the continuing trek to dodge Long Melford's Book Fair traffic, we detoured around towns and managed to get home without getting off the track or lost! Both the small and large, the great and the insignificant, enmesh in this culture which sets great stock in both. For the one so inclined to diversional thought process, that characteristic evokes meditations on bread and flowers. Castles have always meant bread, substance, to the British. Even "Lord," the word for the principal inhabitant of the castle, comes from *Hlaford*, the Old English word for the keeper and dispenser of the bread, the one who has the key to the storeplace of the bread. (Interestingly, it was used first for the wife of the "Lord," or the chieftain.) Such mind excursions connect the castles of antiquity and the likes of Cunobelin, Shakespeare's Cymbeline, with the more contemporary antique shop where the great poet's work in a Leipzig 1843 edition can be bought on a foggy day that invites adventurous meditations. All settles into place as we gain access to the great loaves through the ethereal flower of the hyacinths of the small places, the tea shops, which continue to exude the sustenance of the loaves by the blossom of the environment.

# VII.
# Loaves and Hyacinths in Seaside and Fishing Villages
### ⤙═ *Aldeburgh* ═⤚
### *Walberswick*
### *The Potter's Wheel*

The day we set to explore the seaside and fishing villages, the fog was so thick we decided to delay our departure an hour. We took the opportunity to call home since that endeavor required the availability of some time to wait for the delays and involved conversations with operators. I met the frustrations I expected, but did manage to get a call through to Wilbur, my beloved. The little red phone boxes and their nostalgic associations with World War II provide a study and book treatment in their own right.

Our goal was Aldeburgh, and off we started with my precise map-routing. However, I had mistaken our tea room's name for one in North Yorkshire in a town called Aldoborough. We were almost in Aldeburgh before I realized the error. Being a self-forgiving Navigator-Archivist, and traveling with a non-militant Sergeant Major-Vicar's Wife, we complacently decided to continue on to Aldeburgh, since distances were so short in our British treks, and experience had taught us we usually discovered something of absorbing interest whether we found what we were looking for or not.

Aldeburgh was worth the drive just to go over the berm of cement to face the North Sea, view a fisherman sitting by a beach umbrella, watch a man walking his dog on the beach, and hear the sounds of gulls in the distance.

Norma (SM-VW) had read somewhere that the way to find the best tea shop in town is to follow the little old ladies. We stopped by the side of two gray-haired women who appeared to be out for their morning shopping. Very obligingly, and with expansive gestures, they gave me explicit directions to the BEST one in town, really excellent, they added, and then fell into a discussion about its name. Finally, they cautiously concluded, teeth clicking about the "m," that it was Hemsley's. But they agreed, enthusiastically, it had excellent cakes and sauces, and was just down the street. And, by the way, they added, there was another called The Cabin, and a fine hotel at the "crossroads" called The Wentworth.

We walked up and down the street, and drove it twice, asking for The Hemsley. Three people did not know, one lady said it was The Hammersley, and one shopkeeper came out and directed me to The Cabin, which was really The Captain's Cabin, and not a tea room. We gave up and tried to find the information centre. A person from one end of the street sent me in the opposite direction, and from there, I was sent back. In the middle, a lady, who obviously had become aware of the commotion created in town by two strangers wanting tea, said the tea shop was in the cinema, just "down there." "Down there" turned out to be a former cinema which was being used as a garage for the town ambulance, but was locked. A man in the street said, "Oh, no, it is much further." Undaunted, we followed his directions, and, astonishingly, found a second cinema with the magic blue "i" for information centre, but it was locked with no note or sign indicating when it might open. We did see The

Wentworth, however, in all our excursions through Aldeburgh. It stared at us with its excellence peeking through peeling paint grandeur as we rolled past.

In our dragging Main, or High Street, as it were, by foot and wheel, we did see two items of interest: Lewis House (so indicated over the lintel) and a book stall outside a home, a cart-like arrangement with books on display. In amazement, we watched as a man stopped, examined the books, took one, and dropped money in a container, with no one ever coming out.

As we threaded our way past a red brick (russet, as Henry James would say) wall, a sign announced, "tradesmen's entrance in the lane." (Later, at our farmhouse B&B for the night, our hostess said, as she led us in the back door, "I'll just show you in the trade way and take you to the front where you can bring your car.")

Aldeburgh became significant for the rest of the day's events, and we relished our trip there because of all we found for having gone that way. First, we savored a wonderful drive along the sea to the next town to angle our way back to the highway with the gorse, seeing in the process the quintessential man with his dog, a windmill to the left—all the demonstrative sights to support our phrase, "unspoilt English countryside," which we had started using "'twixt Ipswich and Great Yarmouth." Yarmouth reminded us of David Copperfield's travels, and set me up to give poor SM-VW a discourse on the fact that we were in David Copperfield country in the Aldeburgh area, too.

Our destination was Walberswick, on the sea, below Southwold, another reminder of Old English, with "wold" meaning forest. Our list included two tea rooms there: The Potter's Wheel and Mary's. Both were good finds.

The Potter's Wheel was in an old pottery factory which also housed an art gallery as well as a tea room. The tea room possessed a sea aura: six bleached wood tables, white painted wrought iron chairs, brown tweed carpet. At one end of the shop was a larger table with a lace cloth, covered with cakes and scones. Near the front was one without a cloth which held jams and packaged cakes. Straw racks with two small shelves displayed jams. Because it was located on the green, the North Sea rolled in to its front with hypnotic beauty visible since mists and fogs were beginning to dissipate with the sun. A skylight along the wall was a natural spotlight for paintings for sale. Because of the early hour, we elected to have coffee. With symphony music flowing from speakers back of hanging plants, coffee (and toast—cracked wheat, for me—scone, for Norma) arrived in beige brown turquoise pottery. Wicker shades shielded four ceiling lights. Brown plastic "burlap" place mats carried the earth tones. A black board on the back wall listed menu and prices.

An older couple came in. The woman said to the waitress, "The mist came in quickly." The man, without waiting for amenities said, "One coffee and one chocolate."

We went through the town in search of atmosphere, and found it faster than our pulse: an enormous russet brick house, with about 200 lines running into it, TV antennae posted about, and a wonderful crooked wash line with colored clothes flapping; a scene of fragile beach buildings and hearty beach people, busy about their chores and business, walking, scurrying, bicycling.

# ⊷ *Walkerswick* ⊶

## *Mary's*

We had seen Mary's first, so knew where to find it when we were ready for tea. An expanded home, it offered facilities to eat outside in the garden and looked like a USA picnic table area, except for a few dainty round tables and a Union Jack flying on a pole in the garden's middle.

Prices and teas were posted at the entrance where we learned Mary's offers High Tea. Choices and fares were well-presented: Sausage and Mash; Boiled Eggs, Butter and Bread; Baked Beans on Toast; Grilled Kippers; Fish and Chips; Seafood Thermidor with Salad; Hot Roll and Butter—Choice of Potato.

The shop delighted us because of its sea decor and proximity to the sea. Shells lined one wall above the bench backs interspersed with figures: an old woman mending a sail; a man in a yellow slicker macintosh and whaler's hat; a sailor in navy blue turtle neck and knit cap; a sailing ship made from a cow's horn; a carving of a fisherman's head. Ship paintings and a shadow box decorated the wall. A black and white photograph of a white-bearded man in a flat cap suggested his pink nose though no color emanated from the print.

Some tables were blackish brown wooden trestle tables, looking like school desks, while others had crossed rungs and round tops. People sat on bentwood chairs with dowel backs or on benches with blue-green cushions. Purple, red, and orange throw cushions were scattered about and caught the hue of royal blue napkins. Bright sea colors livened everything to make color and atmosphere independent. We did not have to depend on the splashes of garden brilliance to relieve the muted fog colors we had seen elsewhere.

As we dedicated ourselves to another cup, I said to my colleague, "Suppose our husbands will agree to be donors for the kidney transplants we're going to need after this?" Demarara sugar (coarse-grained, tan, unrefined) was on the table, along with a miniature pottery pot of flowers (one bunch, silk). As we drank from brown and white pottery, we commented that we seemed to be away from the fine bone china. So few miles made such a difference. When life is lived to a smaller scale, changes in style wedge in quickly, or not at all.

Both the waitress and the proprietor continued very chatty, providing much commentary on "the mist." Weather is such a filler for human interaction. What would we do without it? As we sipped (we had decided we must sip and taste, rather than eat and drink), the proprietor took down her wall board to inscribe the menu and prices. I watched her re-hang it, past the mobile of blue fishes and another of blue sailboats. Though amphibious in allusion, the tea room accents dispensed an aroma of hyacinths in the midst of the tea loaves at a place by the sea called Mary's.

## ⊷⊷ *Cromer* ⊷⊷
## *The Buttery*

When we left Spa Farm near Aylsham, we turned north toward Cromer, in spite of the fact that Mrs. Gosling thought we should have gone into Norwich to see the Queen. At Cromer's main intersection we saw another kind of queen: a pink, glowing English mother with two small children, a pram, and two dogs on leashes.

The North Sea unrolled before us just outside of town, with a ship in the distance, on water another stripe of gray-blue with the sky and clouds. We passed The Clifton Hotel and its "Buttery," on the cliff, with only the roadway between it and a drop of several hundred feet to the beach below. True to our adventurous spirit and unbounded willingness to eat at any hour, should the chance arise, we decided to stop in and check it. An OLD, OLD, hotel, it was full of maroon, red, and green in carpets and stuffed furniture. Chairs sported white damask customized arm protectors. Gleaming brass carpet rods anchored maroon stair carpet at each step. Opening to a double stair from the single landing, the stairs framed a huge Flemish appearing painting on the right and a vaulted stained and leaded glass wall on the left. The same style glass circled the lobby and the reception area. A twenty-feet high marble mantel with thigh-high andirons, an antique shoe shine box at its base, and two copper samovars atop, had prominently displayed on it a silver loving cup, engraved "The Tom and Josie White Cup For The Best Dressed Waiter."

Our thought was to check out the "Buttery" for morning coffee, but it was not ready for service. We went on toward Sheringham and stopped at West Runston, at Suzanne's Cake Shop on Cromer Road because we were sensing the American patriotic need of coffee. We had mistaken Suzanne's for a coffee shop; it was a bakery with people in and out making purchases. We threw the manager completely off-stride with our coffee request, but she valiantly offered to make some for us. We agreed she deserved to be a hyacinth, there "amongst" all her loaves, if we granted such titles to people. The Buttery captured our fancy as an ideal location for high tea with its vaunted position overlooking the North Sea and its aristocratic atmosphere that exuded hyacinthian aroma.

## ⊶⇒ *Sheringham* ⇐⊷
## *Pretty Corner Tea Garden*

Sheringham remains in our notes and memory as one of those towns you tuck away, thinking you will make an effort to return some day, knowing you will not, but say as much anyway, being unwilling to say goodbye, and thereby making the departure possible. Part of the charm lay in the unpretentious antique shops. In one, I bought a half handle glass pitcher and glass butter dish. With directions from a policeman who flaunted graying muttonchops whiskers and impeccable manners, we were off to Pretty Corner Tea Garden "at the top o' the hill" in Sheringham Forest.

Encountering the usual frustrations with signs, we took our 50/50 chance of guessing at the way to turn, and with our usual 90/10 record of guessing wrong, got back to the tea garden fairly quickly. Beautifully landscaped and terraced, and with Dutch and Indonesian influence in food offerings, it was a new venture, only five years old when we were there. A house stood near the entry gate. In a land where the buildings are identified by the centuries, the structure on the rest of the property showed its newness. Its car park, a rarity, contained space for five cars. Enough for us! In the fine British custom of understatement, information near the entrance listed five "pleases:"

1. Please keep your dog on lead. Take Doggie Bowls back to the tap on the terrace.
2. Please use waste bins in our gardens and ask for an ash tray if you smoke.
3. Please do not use our sugar spoons in your tea or coffee cups. Teaspoons are provided.
4. Please tell the management if something is not right or failing. We like to know and try to correct it.
5. Tell your friends and neighbors if you have enjoyed your visit and our gardens.

Lights lined walks, surely creating a lovely nighttime atmosphere. A sign announced "trailing geraniums for sale;" other potted plants were visible in the distance along walks toward the pines.

As I was looking at the walled garden near the entrance and the immaculate brick and plaster two-story house, two English couples drove in. One of the advantages of the wanderlust for NKB-Sergeant Major-VW and GSL-Navigator-Archivist was our always being with the English and never encountering tourists. So we had front row seats for observing British character. The women promptly entered, but the men stayed to examine the hood of their gray and red Ford Sierra. One was troubled by the wash job on his car.

I walked around to the dining area: a deck off the "Dutch Country Kitchen" with white tables, brown and white chairs, and orange, brown, and tan umbrellas. The blue flowers on the wall were aubretia. We saw them at Blickling. The same furniture was about a goldfish pool ten feet below the terrace, as well as on the lawns to our back. Cement and crosstie walks bordered with flowers and perfectly edged lawns continued as terraces to the pool level, and back up to the deck area.

We ordered cream tea for one, since we had developed the practice of sharing drink and food to be able to sample more during a "work" day. While we waited, I watched the red-orange fish below me, wondering if they wore that color due to the hardiness of life that close to the North Sea! What a bone-cutting chill the wind has. When our food came, we regretted the single order because we discovered the scone was the BEST one we had eaten in East Anglia. The tractors we saw plowing from the road as we entered ricocheted their sounds through the trees with their turns to add their portion to our total sense involvement in the tea garden visit. While we chatted, we caught views of the sea through Sheringham Forest. The Pretty Corner Tea Garden granted more than a lovely experience; it became a bloom to decorate a memory niche.

*The Owl Tea Room — Holt*

# ⚶ *Holt* ⚶
## *The Owl Tea Room*

Holt left us with an archetype of a breathtakingly beautiful little English village, full of tiny streets, curving roads, and alleys of shops. AND we found a marvelous antique shop and book store which had first and scarce editions; I still have the card with the owner's address:

Simon Gouch Books;
3-5 Fish Hill; Holt, Norfolk

I bought Marie Saunders, my Miltonist friend and colleague, a 1751 edition of *Paradise Lost* "with an engraved portrait and title page and twelve engraved plates—full contemporary calf — joints split." Because names in old books fascinate me, I wrote carefully those inscribed on its fly-leaf:

Thos. Newball Stamford 1758
Lord Cozens-Hardy Gunthorpe
Elizabeth Hepburn

Because I usually buy books for friends and family that I really want for myself, I stood a long time deliberating whether or not I could actually give away the purchase. When I decided I would, I felt extremely generous and virtuous, so I set about looking for an appropriate reward for such a magnanimous spirit. I found it! But, such a book required lengthy rationalizing before final action was taken, all of which adds to the joy of the experience. I deliberated a LONG time, even calling on the resources of SM-VW, herself, no novice at book-buying. Eventually, I bought for myself from Mr. Simon Gouch a *first* edition copy of Thomas Gray's poems with Mr. Gouch's note advising: "1st London edition, 1768, uncut, with original and papers bound in—the first edition was Dublin (now worth a thousand pounds)—later binding with half titles." Without the end papers, the value is less, as addictive book-buyers know. Mine also has the printer's signature, his initial, at the bottom of the page, which is a letter that may run A to Z, or a figure in the tail margin to assure correct assemblage.

We walked around town centre and found The Owl Tea Rooms, a delightful place, just right for Holt, our special village. The front was perfect, even to having their cakes and pastries displayed in view through the white framed widnows. Light and airy, it was decorated in green and white. Furniture was light-colored wood, perhaps oak. Heavy beam supports, light in color, gave the building a sense of permanence. Tables and booths wore cloths of green and white print. The print ran half-way up the wall on two sides, with shelves for china display, and painted green above the shelf. On the other wall, above the beam, was a display of wood irons. Green plants hung about. Ball lamps on green supports and huge paper circles on ceiling lights completed the fixtures.

The shop displayed a wonderful array of breads and pastries. We had Cornish "pastie," a meat and vegetable pie, since it was lunch time, and took two black current tarts with us, along with a cake for our hosts at our B&B.

The name of the shop intrigued me, since the owl from Old English lore did not enjoy a favored spot in metaphorical treatment in literary works. It is usually associated with the lonely, the dark, and the mysterious. A legend about an owl was printed on the back of the menu. I read it with interest.

"Some men of the town Holt, the story goes, caught an owl once and put it in the pound for safekeeping. By the next morning, of course, it had vanished.

"An alternative story is they put it in the great waterspout of the church, hoping that it might drown in the next shower of rain.

"The bird, however, calmly flew up and soared away.

"The people of Holt have ever since been called the knowing ones."

Sergeant-Major-VW and GSL Navigator-Archivist think the people of Holt are the knowing ones because they have Simon Gouch's book store and the The Owl Tea Rooms, such refreshing steps back into Victorian England.

With reluctance, we left Holt and went to Felbrigg, a great house, in the style of Blickling, though not quite as grand. The estate of the Wynham family, it was lovely to view, and we could enjoy a leisurely look because we practically had it to ourselves. Of course, we ended the excursion with a visit to their gift shop and their tea room which exuded a country kitchen kind of effect. Even with the splurge at Simon Gouch's, I found other books at Felbrigg's for the collections of friends.

We took off on a race to get to Cawston and Grey Gables for high tea in a Rectory. With the usual lack of identifying information, we turned back once to ask, but raced up to the door at 4:30, the closing time printed. There we met Mrs. Snaith who told us they were "not doing teas this year—not enough people came." We understood why! Nobody could find her.

At the end of the day, when I deliberated on loaves and hyacinths, the Loaf had to be the Anglo-Saxon beginnings in East Anglia, so vividly brought to mind with the views of the sea, the sea-faring effects, the remnants in the language, and the allusions in the writings. Hyacinths? A Thomas Gray first edition and, The Owl Tea Rooms.

## ·⊶⊜ *Old Hunstanton* ⊜⊶·
# *Le Strange Arms Hotel*

The Le Strange Arms Hotel came to our attention as we traveled from Heacham on north to Old Hunstanton ("Hunston"). Named for a prominent family in the area, the hotel stands by a golf course overlooking the North Sea. An establishment as large and impressive as it is should not have required my usual digressions to seek directions, but when one is a stranger in a strange land, the only recourse remains to stop and ask. The man chosen for our noble purposes gave us what we needed. However, he was out walking his dog Rusty, and he could not engage in his affable conversation with me until Rusty demonstrated appropriately good manners to match those of his owner by sitting in response to the "Sit!" command. Such, Rusty was reluctant to do. My contract in the interaction was to wait patiently until Rusty did sit, which he eventually did. With such cooperation, his owner could turn his attention to my questions. Thus armed, we proceeded to Le Strange Arms, a wonderful old world hotel in an exotic ambiance, which we entered through a partially hidden driveway of gravel that ran alongside the superb lawn. Of Carr stone, the building had urns of flowers in front, and picnic tables on the southeast lawn.

Tea was served in the lounge, a calm, sedate interior in dusty rose and soft blue. Service came in stainless flatware and Dudson-Stoke-on-Trent in England china—white with one black stripe on the top of teapot. Lovely as the tea was, the dominant factor was the place. In a rose and cream pattern upholstery, bordered in blue, chairs sat about white cloth-covered tables, topped with circles of glass. Sofas in blue velvet invited reclining meditations. The blue and pink repeated in flowing drapes and cornices and tie backs over heavy cream lace at the windows. The carved wooden mantelpiece mirrored a matching wood with the corner bar. On the mantel were wooden base lamps, silver *cafe con leche* pots, brass candlesticks, clock, and a landscape of The Broads over all, with shining firescreen and old coal scuttles on the hearth.

Walls were papered in a lower level in white with a plaster-like peach raised pattern, and a softer peach, beige, and gray above. Wallpaper "molding" was brighter peach, gray, and beige. Three painted beams unified the angled walls, the fireplace which pro-truded into room, and the recessed northwest window area. Good paintings graced a lovely setting: river scene, village, country, and two of the Broads. A huge brass urn of ivy sat near the fireplace, one bar stool at the bar, and four lamp fixtures occupied each section created by the beams. A large wooden base table lamp rested behind the sofa where I sat. Magazines lay about the lounge: *Country Life*, *Golf Monthly*. Outside and inside, the North Sea was spectacular, fading into the sky's blue-gray.

To look across the North Sea from East Anglia from such a luxurious setting is to invite meditation on the centuries that sepa-rate the hardy Old English tribes and clans from the waves of marauding Vikings, Danes, Normans, and others who have plun-dered those coasts from the sea. Le Strange Arms offers repose and reflective armament in the aesthetics of hyacinths and teas to defeat the coarseness of the loaves that must be the harsh history of the place.

Farther north, on the sea near Happisburg, we hoped to visit another hotel, The Cliff House, a monastery, and a tea room be-tween the lighthouse and the sea, but it stood "sadly derelict," to borrow a British phrase. We drove around the town once, past the monastery, and up a pebble rock drive to an old hotel, trees finger-laced overhead. The edifice had a look of grandeur, though its thatch roof needed to be repaired. It had the best view in town, on a hill, with the sea on two sides and a lighthouse in the distance. We drove away thinking what a cold and lonely place would be a monastery on this North Sea coast. But the loaves and hyacinths produced by faith are never determined by physical comforts.

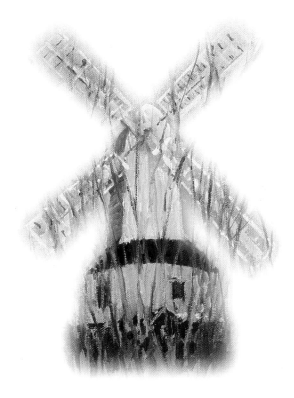

# VII.
# Loaves and Hyacinths
# in River Ports
## ⊶⇒ *Ipswich* ⇐⊷
## *Marlborough Hotel*

We checked into the Marlborough Hotel in Ipswich instead of a Bread-and-Breakfast because we were facing a holiday weekend without a place to stay. Realizing we needed to get settled for the weekend, or sleep in our Keep, the car, we checked our lodging guide for Essex. The Marlborough Hotel in Ipswich had the tea service mentioned for that areā, and seemed a possibility, though we had some concern about vacancies because of its nearness to the sea, the weather granting the first warm days, and people leaving their homes for trips.

From a *fistful of pages* (derived from the map *and* the people we stopped to ask) saying how to get to roundabouts and how many traffic lights beyond, we reached Ipswich Information Centre and . . . it was open. I made arrangements while Norma stayed with the car because of parking problems. The Marlborough was the *only* place we could get in! We took it gratefully. To add to our luck, the management gave us a better price for staying two nights because the season had not officially begun. On Henley Road, the hotel is situated a bit away from downtown and the river port, and looks like an old red brick mansion. To my absolute joy (because of the his-

tory), it sets near Christ Church, Christ Church Park, and Christchurch Mansion, home of Thomas Wolsey, who, though son of a
butcher, became a Cardinal of Rome and all but ruled England while
Henry VIII was "distracted." The Buttermarket, a famous old
building, is here (with a well-known bookshop) and Ancient House,
supposedly once the home of the Chaucers. In addition, the Orwell,
Deben, and Stour Rivers are all near, as well as the coast. We
sensed a good omen in the sign as we drove up: "The Marlborough
Hotel, Cream Teas Served Daily in the Gardens and Lounge, 3:30-
5:30 p.m."

We settled in, then went to "take tea." The trolley was in the
reception area, arranged with three different cakes and scones, a
beautiful ambiance. The room itself posed a double effect, with an
overhang to create a two room illusion. Colors were muted green,
blue, and brown—sofas, brown/green. Wallpaper gave a vertical
illusion of height with columns of poppies in pastel burnt orange
(near tangerine) with a sort of stripe of trellis between. Carpet was
gray and avocado. Wild-life prints hung on the walls. Lamps had
beige shades trimmed in the gray avocado. Wall sconces with small
lamps shed light in needed places. Fresh flowers were everywhere:
in a big straw container, yellow spider mums, yellow daisies, pink
carnations; pink carnations on the mantel; red carnations on a table;
a bowl of daffodils on another table. Palms stood in a glass-enclosed
entry which led to the brass reception desk. Our waiter, who also
helped by carrying in our bags, brought crisp, snowy napkins and a
table cloth when we ordered tea, and set the table with a pretty, but
not exclusive, pattern of a green leaf design on white (England—
Steelite). Our cream came in a silver compote, a bit bent, but with
character, and another held strawberry jam. Coffee, in addition to
tea, and hot water smoked in silver pots. We met the typical British

charm and courtesy we had learned to anticipate from hotel staff and innkeepers. Our manager was chatty: "Sorry the rooms are small. We let the larger ones go first, you know." Our tea was extremely nice and well-presented: scones, thick whipped, not clotted cream, butter, jam, and meringue cake.

We decided to take pad and camera for a walk. Christ Church Park proved to be a treasure with probably 50 acres or more of rolling lawn and trees, some of which had markers naming benefactors who had planted them. Nearer to the "bottom of it," to use the British terminology, stood a monument to nine martyrs. From top to bottom on the marker which was a column about 15 feet in height, a legend read in a circular direction:

The Noble Army of Martyrs
Praise Thee

This Monument is Erected To
The Memory of Nine Ipswich Martyrs
Who For Their Constancy To The
Protestant Faith Suffered
Death by Burning

| William Pikes-1558 | N. Peke-1538 | Agnes Potten-1555 |
| Alexander Gouch-1558 | Kerby-1546 | Joan Trunchfield-1556 |
| Alice Driver-1558 | Robert Samuel-1555 | John Tudson-1556 |

Oh May Thy Soldiers Faithful True and Bold
Fight As The Saints Who Nobly Fought of Old
And Win Them The Victors Crown of Gold
Alleluia

Throughout the park, we were drawn to the various trees planted by people honored with a plaque. I noticed two in particular:

This Oak Was Planted By
Edward Coleby Ransome,
Mayor
On Peace Day, 19. July. 1919

And the same information was communicated for Florence Mitford Ransome, Mayoress.

We went to the back side of Christchurch Mansion, Wolsey's "palace," and walked around it. Massive, red brick, and brooding, it seemed to be still owned by him. The lawns sweep right up to it, and the two wings at front circle out like two arms to form an open court. While I pondered the stormy life and times of Wolsey, I noticed an enormous clock over the front entrance. As I stared at it, the instrument seemed to underline that time really rules in all our struggles, petty or grandiose, Wolsey's or Henry's or . . . mine.

I was still mulling over Wolsey taking on Henry as we left the park and walked on the street to Christ Church, beautiful, but smaller than the Mansion. A woman was trying to parallel park. A young man, her son I decided, occupied the seat next to her. In an effort to match the power mood I was having infused from Wolsey, I stood in the street to direct her. Soon the son jumped out, and we both directed her. The aura dissipated however, as I neared the corner to enter the church yard, and saw across the street a restaurant, Wolsey Kitchen! It did not seem fitting. However, that is the place where my power usually dissipates — the kitchen.

As is true in the other church yards, the tombstones older than 1800 have the lettering worn smooth by the elements. But that fact never dissuaded my persistent graveyard excursions, as NB-SM-VW will attest. The epitaphs both intrigue and motivate my imagination with simply giving names and terse obituary.

George Singleton - 1815
Jerusha - 1816
Jerusha, daughter - 1830 at 19

(I wondered what happened to their six-year-old daughter in 14 years after the parents died.)

John Lea who departed this life Nov. 10, 1805 at 60
Also Mary, his wife Feb, 1809

(How did Mary live during those four years after the death of her husband in pre-Victorian England? Did a son, brother, brother-in-law take her in? How did she survive?)

John Ethan Goff
16 Dec. 1785 at 82
Mrs. Mary Goff
8 Sept. 1786 at 80

(What kind of life did John and Mary have together? Had they been man and wife all their adult years? Were their years together happy? How had they managed to live so long when the life expectancy was much less? Did she really "die" when he was gone, and her body took 9 months to succumb?)

On the wall I noted other resting places:

Robert Minter
d. 12 Sept. 1812 at 31
Also Robert his son who died an infant

(Did Robert the son die of the same cause? What happened to his wife and the infant's mother?)

Back of the yard, in front of the two Roberts were pink, yellow, white, and blue hyacinths blooming: singular heralds to me of an alliance between me and the dead. Was it a coincidence that I, planning a book with hyacinths as a metaphor for the essence of spiritual life, would read the evidence that these people had lived and record their names in my book? I think not. Writers respond to several urges, but the unconscious one, the one that comes as an unarticulated assignment with the calling is the provision of links and connections between centuries, cultures, and individuals. From those intersections arise at least one form of eternal life. What a heavy, yet euphoric, task to be party to creation! What a power to possess the ability to make minds touch in text. Life from death? Whatever God has planned, there is also this. You martyrs in Christ Church Park, you sleepers in Christ Church graveyard, I grant you the eternal life of my text. As long as it lives (and no one will ever be able to destroy every copy of it), you will live . . . and I will live in it with you. I prefer to be pink hyacinths!

We walked back another way to return "home," past shops and huge houses—probably built with the merchant wealth of this area's shipping money and wool trade. On one corner in a Palladian marble facade edifice appeared a neatly lettered sign on the gate and fence: Bethesda Baptist Church. The clock on the front had 1737 on it. Signs closer to the steps announced a goodbye reception for their reverend. Norma thought Reverend Dr. Brown should be recommended, but that his wife should not do it!

We looked forward to a hot tub in the lovely little hotel. In the continuing walk, we discussed such simple pleasures, and then reverted to one of our favorite interchanges: our respective thoughts on how we view loaves and hyacinths.

On our second day in The Marlborough, we gained our laugh for the day, and maybe for the entire trip. We had returned from our Dedham adventure and eagerly opened our silver purchases from the antique fair. I went in to look at Norma's fish knives and forks, saw her flowers from the hotel management, and made disparaging comments about the cultural bias in favor of artists. She went to my room and returned with my little bunch of blossoms she had bought the day before to take a picture. I left to run a bath, and she called the desk to send up flowers to me. She came to my door with the flowers from her gift the day before when I was about to get in the tub and only had on my shirt. I sat briefly to file a nail, and when I heard a knock at the door, I assumed it was she. A bellman bringing the flowers she had asked to be sent up thought the room was empty and came on in. He was shocked, apologetic, and stammered, "I'm so sorry, Madam!" trying not to look below my face. I was hurriedly attempting to get more than two buttons buttoned AND stand short!

# ·›══ *Woodbridge* ══‹·
## *The Ancient House*

After a set breakfast in a dining room at The Marlborough overlooking a walled English garden filled with eye-hurting green and vivid splashes of color, especially the yellow daffodils against the red brick, reluctantly, we left to resume our quest and questings.

A town called Woodbridge and a tea room named The Ancient House comprised our first objective. We started by getting instructions from our nice manager: "Cahn't miss it. Go to the lights — right — take A12 — goes straight to Woodbridge."

We arrived in Woodbridge, but missed the turn he meant, and took the first one, because I was reading to Norma what one of our research books said about Woodbridge: "Ideally, Woodbridge should be approached from the sea, as the first East Anglians approached it, up the beautiful Deben Estuary." The author went on to

*The Ancient House — Woodbridge*

describe an exquisite Georgian village, then added, "The motorist from the south, however, will have been subjected to the horrors of A12 and Ipswich, and the final indignity of Kesgrave, and will have drawn the conclusion that East Anglia is nothing but a long-drawn-out subtopia. He will be refreshed, then, at finding himself in the middle of Woodbridge"

We decided our "hyacinth" for the early morning was to take the turn on a back road, due to my ineptness as navigator, which gave us a splendid view of the river and the flat green with a straight shot into town right past a 16th-century house with an elaborate scroll work sign that said "Noreen Prichard-Carr Teas." We only needed to go around the square and found, about a block down, a parking place in front of the second oldest building in Woodbridge, as we learned later from a policewoman. A Tudor building, now a pub called Ye Olde Bell and Steelyard, it was originally a steelyard, and still had the loft jutting out over the street for the block and pulley hoist.

We walked back to the square to the lower end where Church Street, Miss Noreen Prichard-Carr's street, came in. In the square, sat a statue of Queen Victoria, marked 1887. A couple with their dog on a leash were relaxing in the sun a few feet from the queen's statue. Nearby stood a monument to the war dead: the Great One, 1914-19, and 1939-1945. Names like Grayston, Howard, and Howe walked onto my page as I hurried along.

"The Ancient House" was that. A Tudor building stared back at us through its leaded paned windows that were not diamond shaped, but beveled squares. The three wooden steps leading up from the street were so worn from use that the middle was lower than the sides.

We took our seats at a table for four by the stairway of bare wood steps and carved bannister rails. The white ceiling and pink

walls were beamed and potted plants sat on a white filigreed iron
rack. A *heavy* dark wooden front door boasted longitudinal grooves
all across it and five horizontal rows of studs at intervals interrupted
by a handle door opener rather than a knob.

Coffee and tea were served from a counter by waitresses in red
and white with red sweater vests. A long serving table displayed
twelve kinds of tarts, pastries, tea cakes, and five entire cakes. A
waitress came to us, and suggested we choose which we'd like; we
each took two, which she served, then we shared the four to
sample—a date cake, chewy, chocolate mint, a current cake
(cookie), and another, delicious all. When we paid, we noticed at the
cash register a sign which said, "In future this shop will be closed all
day Wednesday." We wondered why, but dared not ask for fear of
transgressing some basic local wisdom.

Very animated conversations were going on all about us. We
heard two American voices, both women's: one with an English
group to the left on the other side of the stairway, and one to the
right with a group at the window. A man sat at the left table: to the
right, all women. They weren't tourists: Americans at home with the
English? From Mindenhall, the Air Base?

A family of a father, son, and grandmother came in. With the
waitress, the three made a great commotion over choices for the
child, which created pleasant theater for a little one.

Afterward, the father teased with his son.

Joe, the father, said to the child, "Have you got any money?"

"No."

"No?"

Laughter.

Waitress, "Granny's looking after everyone?"

Father, about the food, "Better choice than last week."

A curiosity for us had been the lack of change in places where shoppers buy. The present experience proved no exception. A waitress rushed out for change, people protested they were making a bother, and she demurred, saying that they and the shop next door "do it all the time."

With the tables filled, a young woman drew near us.

"May I?"

"Please do," I answered.

"Thank you, very much."

In fifteen minutes, we knew her history. Her name was Doris Smerling. She lived with her mother in Saxmundham, twenty minutes away by train, took care of her mother, and came to Woodbridge to market each week by train. She always stopped at The Ancient House. She told us about Americans based near her home and commented on how civic minded and helpful they were. The American to our left rose to leave, and Doris stopped her to ask about a mutual friend who had returned to the States. I wondered if the woman's husband or friends were on the Qadaafi raid.

Doris bade us goodbye. We watched her leave and saw others enter. An old couple came in, she in a fur coat—both stooped. He sat and she, very pleasantly, inquired what he wanted, and went for it.

We talked with our congenial waitress, British fair and pink, and inquired about the house. She showed us the bricked in fireplace near the front door with the date in the mantel area—1553. Five tiles were also in the plaster, most with a *fleur de lis* pattern. Miss Noreen

Prichard-Carr had owned the house and run the tea shop for nearly thirty years, living above and having others working for her.

We climbed back up Church Street to the church, St. Mary's Parish Church. I did my tombstone searching for interesting names: Thomas Crimwood died in 1847 at 65; Rosetta, his wife in 1866 at 76 (How did Rosetta live for 20 years after her husband, ten years her senior, died?)

James Pelham, 1765-1850, had a pedestal monument. (Wonder why he was alone? Was he important?)

We went onto the square where a market was being held. I bought a pitcher, beautiful glass, and a sugar dish for 3.50 ($5.53) and 2.00 ($3.16) respectively. A pump in the middle of the square had a Gothic roof over it. I told Norma I wanted Wilbur to build me a Gothic well house. She took a picture of it to show him how to proceed!!

The magistrate, or guild hall, was located at the other end, closer to the Victoria part of the square. As I stood at the booth, paying for my glass, I faced the well, the guild house, St. Mary's House to the right and Peppercorn's Restaurant beside it. In sheer revelry for the moment, I gave each a heart salute.

We were ready to go on to Leatheringham because of a tea room in a mill house we wanted to find. We started right by getting directions from a lovely young policewoman. This is an example of how we travel.

"Excuse me. Can you tell me how to get to Leatheringham?"

"Go through Wickham Market. To get there, turn at the bottom of the street, St. John (a corner is the top of the street, or the bottom of the street—took me a while to understand). Go to the traffic light. Turn left. Follow to another set of lights. Turn left again. Follow to a roundabout (a traffic circle, spewing traffic onto the indicated roads), turn right onto A12. Take A12 to the sign to Framlingham. Take it. Turn off at Leatheringham at its sign. You cahn't miss it."

At the roundabouts, the signs are circular, showing routes possible, and the exit. At the exit, the town name and highway are on a sign which points to the direction of the route. In the country, the signs are easier to decipher, because they point in the direction of the town. They also tell to the quarter of a mile the distance to the town; for example, Leatheringham 2 1/2, Wickham Market 1 1/4. That would be important if we were walking. Town names present fascinating sounds and images: Fernwood Park, Wyndham, Stephen Bayfield, Simon's Cross, Glenering Hall, Saxmundham, Charnwood, Deben, Winston Grange, Fairlawns, Tattingstone. We have quite a collection of names because of the many times we entered unintended destinations. Some of the frustrations of trying to find places relate to trying to understand terminology in direction, by knowing what is meant: (top of the road, bottom of the road — both mean corner, but which corner?) For another matter, road signs are often behind us. That's because they are posted for people in the direction they should be approaching from, and we were always entering from the opposite way.

After the invigorating country drive with views of the grass on the banks of the country lane, bowed walls of red brick about estates, and churches go on and on. Each bow in the wall has a tree presenting a magnificent vista. After three attempts to visit the Leatheringham tea room in a water mill, we learned it was not open yet. But the effort to see it produced some wonderful contacts with the countryside. The quaint mill on the Deben is lovely, evoking for thought George Eliot's fine novel from Victorian England, *The Mill on the Floss*.

# ⊷⟹ *Thorpeness* ⟸⊶
## *The Gallery and The Barn*

As we were leaving Walberswick we realized we had listed a
shop named Eliza Acton on The Old High Road between Yoxford
and Saxmundham, home town of Doris Smerling, our young friend
who had eaten with us at The Ancient House in Woodbridge. We
had discussed her a number of times — her living with her mother,
caring for her, the high point of her week being the train trip to
Woodbridge to shop and have tea at The Ancient House. We had
mentioned her as we passed Saxmundham en route to Walberswick,
and I had commented on how I loved the sound of Saxmundham
and the name of a tea shop, Eliza Acton, in one of our books. We
decided to go back, which is never a problem the way the roads
honeycomb the land, never intruding on village identity, but rather
connecting, connecting, connecting.

The effort to find the Old High Road and the way to Eliza Acton
was reminiscent of attempts to find Hemsley's-Hammersley in Aldeburgh. Two men in a county truck parked on the road could not tell us
where it was, and we discovered it less than 200 feet from them. As
Chief Navigator, I certainly won't ask county men again! Pub person-
nel had turned out to be good instruction sources, we discovered. We
found Eliza Acton with the assistance of one pub manager whose help
I had sought, who had added that it was on the square by the village
church, "a bit more derelict" than most. Perhaps, we suggested to each
other, the men from the county were charged with its upkeep and
couldn't find it! We did find the place, but did not tarry. The only
thing going for Eliza was the name, so we left, in a hurry to get back
to Thorpeness, a wonderful village a mile from good old Aldeburgh. I
had discovered a great sounding shop there from our four or five

sources, and in my duties as Archivist had meticulously kept a record of accidental finds. We were eager to return to check out "The Gallery" at "The Barn" because Thorpeness had a rich, resort look. We had no examples of that ambiance from our initial research.

Amazing what money in the air does: of course, "The Barn" was not readily recognizable—we found a furniture maker's place at the "end of the road," as they say, with "End of the Barn" on his door. We went back to the green, parked, began walking around, and asking. A woman with a dog said she did not know about "The Gallery," but there was a cafe ("kaff") "around there" and pointed in the opposite direction.

We went the way we were headed, and finally disturbed the furniture maker, painty hands and all. He said he thought we were looking for Snape Maltings, which we were not, but did! Then he remembered there was a shop by the "mere" (sailing lake) and directed us back the way the woman and dog had sent us. On the way back up the hill, we passed men from the county working on the road. One said, "Lovely for you this morning, my dear," just as gallant as you please, but I did not ask him the way to "The Gallery."

We got "to the top of the road" and there it was—next to the boating lake, garden overlooking "the mere," as the Guide said. "The Barn"was even painted on the end of the building. Nobody told us there were two barns.

The Gallery, strategically located by a beach, had an inside shop and display area for paintings—primarily sea scenes, but there was also a lovely water color of Leiston Abbey ruins. With nautical decor, brown carpet, dark woods, and armless captain's chairs, it had white and blue walls in the different areas. A nice lawn rolled out from the back, but the front lawn was equipped for service. As a terrace from

*The Granary Tea Shop*

which to view the "mere," a brick wall enclosed the outside dining area. In gray bricks, the wall had a battlement effect with intermittent three-brick-high raised areas. In the garden middle stood a column with the shop's sign at the top, supported by wrought-iron scroll work at its base with a round circle of flowers, and beyond that a brick tile circle like the walk's composition. In the center of each garden half, with the column and walk making the half division, pedestal planters maintained a watch over the other plants like sentinels. Eight to ten tables, mixed wooden picnic and white metal, were scattered about the area.

Among the tables, mallards strutted, in spite of their begging, in their gray morning suits with the bit of blue lining showing under their wing tips, red brown shirt fronts, white and green neckties, and orange boots. Sergeant-Major Brown, the Vicar's Wife, pointed to the dowdy brown ones, waiting disconsolately at the sign circle, and commented, "Their wives."

Navigator-Archivist Lewis responded, "They are that color from drinking too much tea."

The lawn beyond the wall was sliced by the road, but continued on the other side, running around a tiny circle lake, a pool, actually, before it tacked onto the lake pier. In the midst of such a peaceful setting, I became aware of jets flying over every 2-3 minutes and tried not to think of the Halls of Montezuma or the Shores of Tripoli or the marines or any other figure more military than Sergeant-Major Brown, VW.

## Snape Maltings
## The Granary

Intrigued by the furniture maker's comments about Snape Maltings, we decided to "search it out," when we discovered The Granary Tea Shop in one of our listings. Part of a collection of 19th-

*Bridge House Tea Rooms — Brandon*

century buildings on the bank of the river Alde, the area has a world
famous concert hall (the spring program offered "The Coronation of
Poppea," by Monteverdi, and Verdi's "La Traviata"), shops, galleries, and activity holidays. The latter phrase was a new term to me,
but its description sounds like a variation on American summer
camps; references were made to tuition for a center for crafts, arts,
and studies in the Suffolk countryside. For example, participants
learned skills in bobbin lace-making, samplers, machine patchwork,
and stitching; Suffolk countryside characteristics in spring and
flowers of the Suffolk coast, exploration of Suffolk towns and villages; bird study, including song, recognition, and migration tracking; and introduction to watercolor art, screen-painting, etching, and
landscape painting.

In the old granary, The Granary was ours, after the usual adven-
tures and misadventures with road signs. It was behind and to the
side of the Plough and Sail Pub, where three men were being served
outside on the porch as we drove up. A Dalmatian lay at the feet of
one of them.

The Granary looked the way it sounded: warm brown wood and
white walls, tables, booths, chairs, service at one end with food
spread buffet style in covered containers on a service bar atop a
brick wall about three feet high that divided dining from service.
Paintings about the wall were for sale. Picnic tables waited in front
where I sat to write near a woman eating and close to people exiting
an alley which ran between two sets of buildings.

We stopped during our third trip through Saxmundham for the
day ("'Allo, Doris!") to buy gas at our favored Four Star supplier.
That particular one was also a garage with an actual repair shop.

Sergeant Major, VW, returning, said, "We need to be careful.

Three cars in this repair yard were smashed on that curve right there to Great Yarmouth."

GS Lewis, Navigator-Archivist replied, "The drivers were high on tea."

## ⋙ *Brandon* ⋘
## *Bridge House Tea Rooms*

We had on our list the name of a shop in Brandon, a town located on the Little Ouse River. With minor difficulty, and only one stop in the town at the post office, we found it, just over the bridge, and at the bottom on the bank of the Little Ouse.

We loved its look immediately—its sign in GOTHIC lettering of "Bridge House Tea Room" hanging from the front—beautiful red door with a ring handle—a three tunnel bridge, people outside on the river bank at picnic tables—stained glass signs with Tea House lettering.

Inside, the antique look won our hearts—heavy and light bare wood—non-matching, but all quite beautiful—tables with huge, ornate legs, one of the tables having a towel pole along its side.

An enormous solarium, the tea shop, maybe 50 X 50 feet, was filled with antiques, especially stained glass windows of all kinds, and most of them were for sale. Hanging plants and others stood about on every free surface. Stone wear pottery in earth colors accommodated violet, dark maroon dried arrangements. Transoms all around the windows repeated a leaf, flower, or swag design in leaded opaque, color, and clear glass. A white ceiling fan sat unmoving over it all.

Menus contained verses from "The Owl and the Pussycat." Ours read: "So they sailed away, for a year and a day, to the land where the bong tree grows, and there in a wood a piggy wig stood, with a ring at the end of his nose." A picture of a pig decorated the cover.

In front of the establishment, on the river's edge, two soldiers, British, were having tea. At one point, they came in for more hot water. A mina bird, a loud one, kept up its calls in the background.

Sue Kilty, the proprietor, came out to speak with us. She and her husband had lived in London, but finally left because of the race riots. When the house came on the market, she and her husband bought it five years before our visit. They put in the business and she has an antique shop with it, specializing in stained glass repair. People all over England call her with old windows for sale. She buys them for a hundred pounds or so, repairs them, and sells them to dealers who come up from London, as well as others from other markets.

Mendenhall, a big US Air Base, is nearby. We asked her about the attitudes toward Americans. She said relations had been good until the Qadaafi bombing, but became strained because American tourists were staying away. "The attitude is," she said, "it's all right to bomb from our bases, but not to come here with us." She had an American flag with the British one on the flag pole, to make a state-ment, she said.

Brandon is a town which falls and rises. Once it was the flint source of the world. The bridge and buildings all are built with flint stone. Before modern weaponry, its flint was highly prized. With the advent of gunpowder, the economy collapsed. Then the citizenry rebuilt their economy with fur—rabbit fur—and the London market was called Brandon. In the '40s, disease wiped out the rabbits. "Now we're into Americans," she said, smiling.

The drive to and from Brandon was especially nice through tall pine woods with the English haze beyond their trunks and hovering in layers of wisps on the meadow that was visible.

# ⟶ *Reedham* ⟵
# *Briar Tea Room*
# *Moulton St. Mary Church*

On some occasions in life, we must discuss what did not happen in order to explain that which did. Our first goal one morning entailed a trip to Reedham and the Briar Tea Room because the shop, situated on the River Yare, reportedly flourished with a good waterside atmosphere. However, unexpectedly, the FIRST HYACINTH of the day came with a turn around a bend from Damgate to Freethorpe, and we both caught our breath at the sight of a perfect farm beside its own perfect church with *its* own perfect Norman tower, complete with celtic cross in the graveyard. Of course, we hopped out . . . Norma, with her camera, and I, with my notebook. From the farm gate with royal blue paint under peeling green paint behind anemic weeds to the celtic cross memorial to the war dead of Moulton St. Mary (the church/community), I sensed a magnetism I could not name.

> "To the Glory of God and
> in Grateful Remembrance" it said,
> "Their names liveth forever."

On one side was "1914-18" and "1939-45" on the other (the north) away from the sun, where the mossy cover was greener on the names inscribed from WWI:

> John L. Cator—Norfolk Regt.
> Eric J. Coose—Stoker Regt. Norfolk
> On the legible side, these were listed from WWII:
> George Adams—Norfolk Regt.
> William R. Ecclestone—Norfolk Regt.
> Sergeant Harry A DuRose—Norfolk Yeo-y
> Herbert J. DuRose—Norfolk Yeo-y

2nd Lt. Bertie R.W. Chapman — S. Lancer Regt.
Horace W. Shorten — R. Fusiliers

While I stood reading the names, a breeze fluffed my hair on the left, and, simultaneously, I heard a jet fly over and birdsong. I looked up at the vapor trail in the faded, washed denim sky and caught a sight at the same time of the colors on the church roof: dark red and purple on the gray-black of the tower; red-brown in the center nave; and the apse, black and purple-blue. My line of vision dropped onto the curving wall of red brick, contrasting with the Norman pebble mortar of the church. I glanced around at the gravestones, saw the one of Edward Rising Boult who died in 1880, leaning the way a grave-stone should, and wondered if he had loved his church as much as I did in that moment. Nellie Wymer and Frances Rosa Myhill lay on the other side of me, among, but apart from, all the rest. Had they found all they needed here? Would I? Do any of us, anywhere?

Reedham was a place of vibrance and activity. A working, hurryng little river, the Yare, produced a businesslike current proving itself by the duck at labor to stay still by the bank against its force. Its width did not suggest the depth that would be necessary for the size of a blue and white ship at anchor on the side. Boats rested alongside at marinas. Others sliced along the river, ducks swimming along behind. Like British dogs, British ducks have seemed very sociable everywhere we have gone, apparently imitating the impeccable manners of the country. A clean, black top road ran between the marina and houses lining it behind dainty gardens. Reeds grew right to the water's edge. Bunches were stacked farther away on the opposite shore. We recalled we had passed a house being thatched. Everywhere, people were walking well-behaved dogs on leashes. I saw only one free dog during our odyssey. He was on a beach and showed his good manners by bounding along as though on a leash, very close to his master, as if he were saying, "See how well I behave — see how wise you are to trust me."

We found the Briar Tea Room without any problem, but it was not open except on Sundays, so we had to cross it off our list since we planned to be in another district by Sunday. But we did return the next day because NKB, SM-VW, had serious doubts about her camera and film performance when she was shooting the pictures of the exquisite little church at Moulton St. Mary, and GSL-NA, had bought a FIRST EDITION of Thomas Gray's poems the previous afternoon, among them, "Elegy Written in a Country Church-Yard." My special empathy with the book has to do with my churchyard fascination. Gray's "Elegy" had been on my mind every time I walked into one and meditated on the lives, who the people were, how they lived. That feeling I sensed the day before with the breeze, jet, and birdsong enveloping me with life in the presence of death, with the secrets of life locked in the graves, seems exactly what he describes. And to come upon a first edition! I will do without something else to make up for what I have done.

We started the day, early, with a trip back toward Reedham to the Moulton St. Mary Church. I read the Sergeant Major VW "Elegy Written in a Country Church-Yard" en route. Upon arrival, and before our reverence, I took my FIRST EDITION into the churchyard and we read a selected passage there:

> The curfew tolls the knell of parting day,
> The lowing herd wind slowly o'er the lea.
> The plowman homeward plods his weary way,
> And leaves the world to darkness and to me.
> Now fades the glimmering landscapes on the sight,
> And all the air a solemn stillness holds,
> Save where the beetle wheels his droning flight,
> And drowsy tinklings lull the distant folds —
> Save that from yonder ivy-mantled tower
> The moping owl does to the moon complain
> Of such, as wandering near her secret bow'r,

Molest her ancient solitary reign.
Beneath those rugged elms, that yew-tree's shade,
Where heaves the turf in many a mouldering heap,
Each in his narrow cell forever laid,
The rude forefathers of the hamlet sleep.
    Some village-Hampden, that with dauntless breast
    The little Tyrant of his fields withstood;
    Some mute inglorious Milton here may rest,
    Some Cromwell guiltless of his country's blood.
Far from the madding crowd's ignoble strife
Their sober wishes never learned to stray;
Along the cool sequestered vale of life
They kept the noiseless tenor of their way.

American tourists might look askance at a couple of women in tennis shoes in a 12th-century church graveyard, reading poetry to a bunch of grave stones, but none of the English passersby seemed to notice. The reverie and contemplation produced by our act, coupled with my friend's encouragement to return and read there endear her to me forever. Sergeant-Major bought the Vicar, hers, some books by a parson. She commented that titles relate to city and country and one chapter dealt with his views about churchyards.

We read a sign inside the porch entry that the church is no longer being used, but is still "consecrated." (Sounds like some of my "talents.") I padded off to a barn where there was noise to ask about the church and was told the key could be gotten by checking with the Manor Hall Farm next door or the Vicor in Acle or Beighton. I could not rouse anyone at Manor Hall Farm, so I recorded the information that was on the church door. Someday, we must find out about that little church. Place, formation, endurance, meaning: the yeast of the loaf perseveres. Emotion, senses, companionship, symbol: the beauty of the flower interprets.

*The Olde Tea Shoppe — Lavenham*

# IX.
# Loaves and Hyacinths
# in Wool Villages

*⇒⇒ Lavenham ⇐⇐*
*The Olde Tea Shoppe*

W e worked our way to Lavenham, a jewel of a medieval town, with two styles for taking tea: one, the cozy tea room, and the other in the Swan Hotel in the grand, high tea manner. With twisting, turning, and back-tracking, we covered Stowmarket, Finborough, Hitcham, Preston, Kettlebaston, Bildeston, and Monks Eleigh to get to Lavenham. Breathtaking, it looks like something Walt Disney created. Regarded as the finest survivng example of a medieval town, it boasts its superb ancient buildings. The medieval street pattern still exists with its market place, and more than 300 buildings are on the architectural and historical interest list.

Across the road from The Olde Tea Shoppe is the magnificent church of St. Peter and St. Paul with its splendid tower arch. The DeVere porch was paid for by the 13th Earl—his arms are all over it. The bells, eight, are famous. The tenor, weighing a ton, is said to be the sweetest bell in England. Lavenham portrays a prime model of the wool villages of the 15th century.

The tea shop looks like Geppetto's house with its beamed ceilings, uneven walls, lamps by the broad fireplace overhang, and potpourri in pomander bags. It also evokes a Victorian ambiance with the beige, dark rose, and brown small print in tablecloths, rose carpet, brown and white dishes, mobile at the window of miniature baskets of flowers. Perhaps most notable was an overarching, pervasive quiet that seemed different from other places we had visited, in spite of our being there at lunchtime. Possibly, the tranquillity emanated from the church across the road which did dominate the setting. Or maybe it was the step back into a past era. But a pastoral peace pervaded both place and people.

Because it was lunch time, and we experienced tea saturation at the moment, we determined that was the place to indulge truly our British initiation with sample steak and kidney pie. The dish was very flavorful, but the huge, luscious pastry crust may have helped! As we ate, I engaged in my favorite activity: people watching. An older man, eating alone, reading, was having his ale. A couple, very English, sat at the window with the church in the background.

SM-VW patiently waited while I gratified my graveyard-visit obsession after we investigated the church. During our wanderings through the inspiring architecture, we chatted with a friendly couple who said to us, "We knew someone who went to Oklahoma . . . ah, no, Colorado . . . well, where the cowboys are." Because we enjoyed The Olde Tea Shoppe so much, and because we were still in the vicinity after we looked for a B&B and checked out the towns of Hadleigh and Sudbury, we returned there for tea. While we sat by the window and reviewed the day, I scrutinized the church and the graveyard, that time knowing I looked across a host of others who had owned this life before us: Hannah Elliston, who departed this life, January 20, 1881; Betsey Turner, who fell asleep November 21, 1883; Robert Johnson, who died August 7, 1815; Samuel Turner, 1735; and others whose departure date was obliterated by time's scouring brush on their grave stones. The return provided an opportunity to chat with the proprietor of The Olde Tea Shop, a charming young man who had bought the place the previous year. I thought of our encounters with young men in managerial positions of small businesses in quiet places where there is great movement, such as Andrew Hodson at The Market Place in Framlingham, as opposed to women managers of the busy businesses in more quiet locales, like Sue Kilty at Brandon's Bridge House Tea Rooms. Perhaps the observation is based in coincidence, but the situation seems quite apparent.

The Olde Tea Shoppe and Lavenham are both loaf and hyacinth: the stalwart endurance and the aesthetic expression grant evidence of that durability. The day's excursions presented to me another place that extracted the same reverence for place, person, life, death: Hitcham. Hardly a wide place in the road, Hitcham is an old wool town near Bildeston. Its importance for me, grave visitor that I am, resides in its being the burial spot for John Henslow, a nineteenth-century teacher. He angered local farmers by starting country schools and teaching inflammatory subjects like botany, so viewed because they rendered people unfit for their stations in life. At a later time, he redeemed himself in public opinion by finding a use for Suffolk Crag, the deposits of fossilized fish dung which is a productive source for phosphate fertilizer. As botanist, naturalist, and teacher, he had great influence on one of his students, Charles Darwin. Henslow feared Darwin would develop doubts about Genesis if given Lyalls *Principles*, a radical book of the day, but was honest to do so, trusting in Darwin's piety to remain above doubts. Doubts did come, as did *Origin of the Species*. From a person who lies at rest in a village of a few clustered buildings, in a church with fifteenth-century angels on its screen carrying the instruments of the Passion, came seeds for humanity's thought revolution. *The power of the educated mind: the free mind:* loaf and hyacinth!

If Hitcham presented reverie, Hadleigh provided the day's laugh. A gentleman, whom I selected for my "instructions-for-the-day" list and who helped me on the street at Hadleigh with directions, said, "I admire you Americans. Can't im-AH-gine cancelling your holidays like you are. It's safe here. But Mr. Reagan did right. Cahn't let those AHsses (asses) go round blowing up things."

We loved Lavenham so much that we elected to spend our last day in East Anglia there. What a good decision that was! The "finest 15th century town" in England was aswarm with people: couples, families, all out to enjoy the Sunday . . . and perhaps the bank holiday the next day. Earlier, when we could separate ourselves from The Olde Tea Shoppe, we discovered three other lovely tea shops: the Swan Hotel, a wonderful old Tudor building, The Old Chapel Tea Room in the Guild Hall, and The Bank House Tea Shop. We decided to *end it all right there* (50+ tea shops!) with a sample visit to the Bank House Tea Shop and a traditional tea at the Swan, which we did so after a walk about town, and a sketch and reading time.

Lavenham is its own time machine—makes Disney appear a realist. Disney did not really create all that fantasy. He just visited Lavenham and drew it the way it is: pink-timbered, crooked houses with slanting floors and undulating roof lines, leaning over the street. On High Street, one "block" from Market Place, Market Cross, Guild Hall, was this announcement:

"487th Bomb Group
USAF
Returns to Lavenham 9-12 May, 1986"

"Veterans of the 487 who flew from Lavenham Airfield in World War II are re-visiting Lavenham. On Sunday, May 11, they will lay a wreath in the Market Place at 11:30 a.m. Afterwards they will be entertained at a buffet lunch in the Guild Hall. It is hoped that the people of Lavenham, particularly those who lived here 1942-5 will come along to renew old friendships. (3.50 a person — 11:30-2:00)"

Strange. I felt a closeness again to John Appleby, my Arkansas "neighbor" whose rose garden we had visited at Bury St. Edmunds. I had sensed several contacts with the historical aspect of the area that day: being a student of Old English beginnings in East Anglia; a daughter of the region's Puritan tradition; a spiritual ex-patriate of the mother culture, an American coming home to roots; a child of WW II memories; and a US regionalist with John Appleby (who had obviously discovered something of himself in East Anglia, as I had done), with whom I shared Arkansan heritage through my mother's family beginnings there. How I wish I knew more about Mr. Appleby. He is a hyacinth in my bouquet, and my metaphysical contacts with him through Bury St. Edmunds interests and Arkansas progeny allow me to reach out and take his hand, though my fingers close on themselves.

## ⟶ *Lavenham* ⟵
## *The Bank House Tea Shop*

We took morning tea at The Bank House Tea Shop (on High Street) which had an Egan Ronay card in the window. The shop illustrated what had become typical: white on green cloths, and green on white covers atop that; Steelite stoneware (white with a maroon band); beige on brown carpet; small square room, light wood furniture (7 tables X 4 chairs); and quilting (patchwork) displayed for sale, primarily bags and pillows in windows, corners, on the wall. Family groups sat in the moving swirl. To my right was a handsome couple, 50-ish, she in a pink and white angora golf cap, pink pants, and white sweater, obvious in their enjoying each other. Behind them, a younger couple exuded the same kind of happiness. Perhaps we had become so

British in our absorption in our tea pilgrimage, we simply settled back and savored being a part of the scene.

## ⤜⟶ *Lavenham* ⟵⤛
## *The Swan Hotel*

A different air surrounded the hotel. The Swan Hotel had scaffolding up and was acquiring a new roof. It had been expanded, but a good job was done in retaining the flavor of the 14th-15th-century building, even to the "new" champfered beams. One antique pendulum clock, like the one at The Angel Hotel in Bury St. Edmunds, marked time near the entry, and another continued the work in the room where we sat. Taste and aesthetic presence radiated from the dark carpets, the dark red and cream-colored cut-velvet patterned upholstery, and single white carnations on the tables. Everything carried the musical gloss of that wonderful sound of low, muted murmur of English voices.

" . . . always somebody else . . . "

" . . . not really . . . "

With no small degree of nostalgia, we lifted a high tea menu for the last time:

Menu: Traditional English Tea (for one and one tea—our order)
    2 hot fruit scones
    2 home made cakes
    sandwich selection (cucumber, tomato, egg, salmon)
    butter
    strawberry preserves
    whipped cream
Tea: China, Assam, Darjeeling, Lord Grey (We chose Assam.)

*The Essex Rose*

We sat and absorbed our last tea in East Anglia in the wonderful old wing back chairs, eating from Wedgewood Insignia (we had *that* at the Piccadilly Hotel in London) and silver pieces, looking at wall cabinets with antique dolls, stuffed birds in front of a mirror above a high back carved bench (maybe from a church) and hearing, " . . . I was told . . . ," " . . . marvelous . . ." Without speaking, we nodded our agreement. Satiated with loaves and inebriated by our bacchanalia with hyacinths, we had found the fitting way to close our parenthesis on East Anglia.

# Dedham
## The Essex Rose

Our travel route into Dedham provides an overview into the way I navigated as Navigator-Archivist. Driving on the left without pullover spots or shoulders for pausing, SM-VW, my Driver-ess, was at my mercy once we started. And because there were no parking places, she had to stay with the car either to pause discreetly or keep circling while I hopped out to get instructions. We should have taken the Ipswich turn to go to Dedham, but that seemed wrong to me, not realizing there was a "roundabout" just off the "dual carriageway" that led on south. Sooo, we had a scenic detour across the River Orwell (Hello, George!) and turned around. However, there was a way to get back to A137, which is the Norwich Road that we could have taken back to our "mini-roundabout" to Valley to Henley to the Marlborough Hotel, but didn't know! (Whew!) A137 did get us to Manningtree and on to Lawford to the gas station (where fresh cut flowers were on sale) to the air pump (for the tires) to the nice man at the counter for instructions to the pub on the right (one more mile) to the Dedham sign which advised that Dedham lay three miles ahead. My Driver-ess, the SM-VW, is Exhibit A of the fact that patience does exist in this world and is truly a virtue to be cultivated. As we entered the Dedham Vale, another sign said, "Please take your litter home." By that time, we had a sack full in our travel instructions; we always took it home.

Dedham Vale, Constable country, is hallowed ground to an artist. The lane was as it should be: thatch houses, tall trees, bark, moss-covered. An elderly woman strode along with her cane. Norma paused to show me the first glimpse of Dedham's church tower through the trees and past the countryside; Constable painted it from that spot and made it famous. In repayment for all the times she had shared my moments of silent obeisance before some historic or literary geographical heart shrine of my own, I sat meditative, too.

Dedham was hosting an antique fair when we arrived, the one Patricia Macgregor in Framlingham's Tiffin Tea Room could not attend because of her "unwell" dog and lack of "transport." We decided to attend in her place. We went first to the antique show at the upper end of town, past the war dead monument, the square, and the church. We did stop inside the church, another glorious product of the wool villagers's piety, before seeking the whereabouts of the fair. Because old silver is so interesting and readily available, we often stood for lengthy periods before silver displays reading the silver marks, the periods, and creating fantastic narratives for the journey of the pieces from their owners to the show cases. I could no longer resist the "bargains," so I bought a few items: tongs in Sheffi-eld Silverplate by J. Prime, 1839, with seals and marks, 5 pounds ($7.90); tea caddy in Old Sheffield Silverplate by N. Hutton, and a tea scoop, either Georgian or early Victorian, 8 pounds ($12.64); silver spoon with the initials CW, Sheffield, 1907, Edwardian (Edward VII), 4 pounds, 50 pence ($7.11); and a silver spoon, initial G, Dublin 1814, Georgian (Geo IV), (the Dublin assay office closed in the 1970s), 8 pounds ($12.64). Norma bought fish knives and forks, the catalyst for the flower incident at The Marlborough. Feeling the pride of ownership, we marched resolutely away from the fair before we were more of an economic boost than we could afford to be. However, at London's Covent Garden antique fair, I lost control again: soup spoons with my initial (1890s), a small flat fork (1920), a medicine spoon (1870), a larger flat fork (1870), tea knives (1890), my name on a Victorian pin (1870), and a toast rack (1910).

The stellar attraction to Dedham, for our tea enterprise, was The Essex Rose, a large shop located off the square across from the church. The menu, which I asked to buy, and the hostess gave me, has a charming picture on the cover of a woman at tea, some history of tea ("tea was discovered by Emperor Shen Wung in 2737 BC, which was just about the time Noah was setting off in the Ark"); kinds (Ceylon, Earl Grey, Darjeeling, House Blend); and the menu: 5 choices. We ordered a pot of tea, scones, and choice of two cakes, which we then shared: eclair, coffee, chocolate, Victorian (creamy).

While we waited, we watched Dedham life out the big window. The most interesting incident occurred when a man with a large, handsome dog stopped, removed the animal's leash, and told his pet to go bathe in the mill water. When finished with his ablutions, the dog returned, the man bent to dry him, re-snapped the leash, and the two resumed their walk.

If Lavenham's Old Tea Shoppe was the most appealing to us, The Essex Rose became the most spectacular. Its atmosphere was country British with all the charm that phrase suggests. Larger than most places we visited, it occupied an entire house, with the upper floors dedicated to living quarters from time to time, as we were told. The dining room was really three rooms in a row which opened into each other. We were seated in the middle one, but could see clearly both of the other two sections past the candle sconces. Enormous beams, beveled in two places near us, white walls, leaded windows in irregular shapes, board floors, and dark wood tables with bentwood chairs for two or four, as well as booths, defined the dining area. Blue and white plates on the wall at one end, prints on the walls opposite the windows, a couple dozen kitchen witches hanging from one beam, and wrapping paper on a six wire rack in floral and animal motifs signaled the grander business scale of The Essex Rose.

The tea food was beautifully presented; tiny candied orange slices and strawberries adorned the cakes. Our tea was served in Lord Nelson pottery, handcrafted in England since 1758, fittingly, a rose pattern with green and blue leaves and a classic Roman block design around the borders. Mr. Dell Brower, the proprietor, stopped to talk with us. With ease and charm, he seated himself and chatted as though the three of us were longtime friends, newly reunited to discuss events of mutual interest. He openly approved of "our lack of fear of terrorism" as attested by our presence in England at that particular time, and told of greater danger when he visited Los Angeles after the Watts riots. He said he was glad the bombers went after Qadaafi, that it didn't bother him a bit that the bases and the bombers fulfilled that duty, that they bothered him more when they flew over the golf course and disturbed his golf game. Ever the genial, articulate host, he talked about the shop, The Essex Rose, in response to our questions. He told of its being a 15th-century build-ing, first used by Flemish weavers, immigrants for the wool business, then, its service to house the ironmongers, and finally, its existence as a tea shop. I asked him for an interview and for an appointment time to return to talk to record his comments when he was less preoccupied with business. He agreed readily. When Mr. Brower turned his attention to his other guests, we looked at our plates. I commented, "I'm beginning to understand why there are not tea room books."

Norma added, "Researchers died in the process."

At that, we lapsed into one of our frequent insider word pun exercises. For example, "How does 'O.D.' relate to tea drinking and driving?" Answer: "It can mean 'overdose' or 'overdrive.'" We could also create proverbs. For example, "If the roundabouts don't get you, the tea will."

Having finished, we walked across the square, as Mr. Brower had directed, to the information center for materials on Constable, and proceeded on to the weavers's houses, obviously a kind of 15th-century segregation arrangement for imported cheap labor. Of course, I slipped into a reverie on George Eliot's *Silas Marner*. Naturally, I had to check out the grave yard—we were told at The Essex Rose there are Flemish names there because of the weavers; a woman was busily putting out jonquils on graves. We strolled across the green and saw one of the humorous British signs we had grown to love; "The fouling by dogs of these pitches or the children's play area is offensive." (We wondered if the dogs could read.)

Back at the square we were stopped in our tracks at the war dead monument, an obelisk 15-20 feet above a circular stone bench. The legend announced: "In Honour of Dedham men who died in the service of their country and in the cause of freedom 1914-1919 and 1939-1945.

"We that survive perchance may end our days in some employment meriting no praise. They have outlived this fear and their brave ends will ever be an honour to their friends."

## 1914-1919

Ernest George LaneFrank Albert Sage
Edward Ogg                    Albert Sharp
Birtie Osborne               George Sharp
Leonard Passival             John William Smith
Alfred W. Radford            Albert Henry Walby
Robert James Rant            William H. Watson
Alfred Rudge                 Gerald W. Watson
Fred Henry Winney

(On one of her painting trips to this area, Norma had stayed with a Mrs. Watson. We wondered if William and Gerald were her kin.)

## 1939-1945

Frederick G. Barber          Bertie A. Garrod
Leonard Beard                John Raymond Howe
Edward Bland                 Henry W. Polson
John Bland                   Russell H. Smith
Leonard C. Clover
Dominick F.G. Dalton

### Civilians:

Thomas F. Denney             Joan A. Coomber
Frederick A. Dines           Bob Coomber
Leslie F. Eagle              Leonard E. Francis

(Were they hit in one of the lookouts?)

Our thoughts swirled at the possibilities posed by the names: the loss suffered by families (especially those with multiple deaths), the community, and the nation as the totals mounted in considering such monuments throughout the numerous sites where such existed to memorialize and create memory.

We took off to retrace our tracks "home" to The Marlborough

with intentions to return the next day for the interview before turning north. Along the road to A137, we met seven horseback riders,
replete with riding hats and crops. Just a few miles from that sight, a
pheasant flew up and almost hit the car.

We drove all the way to the mini-roundabout without incident,
but I hesitated momentarily and we overshot it. However, we were
able to circle and get back on Valley to go to Henley, our way
"home." Only once did we have to turn around in a driveway: at a
place with the house name "Gresham Court."

Norma said, "We've been here before. Remember Gresham
Court?" With our customary readiness to take an insignificant event
and make it greater, we began to play with her comment. We decided it was a great line for a mistake or a need to retrace on this
trip, or even a fine book title: *Remember Gresham Court?*

Back at Dedham the next day, we drove around the mill, saw the
weavers's cottages again, and kept our recording appointment with
Mr. Dell Brower at The Essex Rose. When we finished, he walked
to the street with us and pointed out other places of interest. Quite
casually, he gestured two doors from The Essex Rose, "That is the
house of Thomas Sherman, forefather of your General Sherman.
Some of them were writers. Two of the sons went to America. They
were very prolific. People keep coming here to trace their family."
Norma and I exchanged wide-eyed glances. "My maiden name is
Sherman," I said. Mr. Brower seem shocked, then excited. "Then
here are your roots. Or maybe your forebears came from Bungay
and Eye. The family was also there." Reluctantly, I confessed that I
had never tried to trace my family.

## ⊷ *Sudbury* ⊶
## *The Old Bull*

Sudbury, birthplace of Gainesborough, boasts a statue of the famous painter and his palette in front of the church on Market Square. The weaving tradition continues in the town, and the silk wedding dress of Diana, Princess of Wales, was woven in Sudbury. Many Georgian buildings grace the streets. Early in our travel, we stayed the night in a medieval building called The Old Bull, an inn that had been a pub at one time. A bull dominates in the DeVere coat-of-arms, the same family that built the DeVere porch in Lavenham's church. Owned and run by Judith and Roy White for six years when we were there, he is a policeman, and she is the Bed-and-Breakfast manager. Before that, it stood empty seven years; "It stood derelict," as Mrs. White said.

So much about The Old Bull intrigued us. A framed copy of the "indenture," an early deed, was hung prominently. We learned that the term comes from the indented way two copies are cut apart. In earlier eras, a legal agreement would be copied twice, with one part for each party, so each could prove ownership of the correct deed because of the "indenture," the way the two fit together. A note below the frame informed that there were no deeds prior to the one of the frame dated 1834, July 10, which began, "Document of Indenture, 1834, July 10, Stephen Spurgin of Sudbury and the county of Suffolk Plasterer and Innkeeper William Elliston and Robert Burrows, . . ." Stephen Spurgin remained Mine Host of The Bull for most of the middle 19th century.

Other items of historical interest were displayed; a picture showed a flood around the Inn with a police sergeant Lander, standing in front in an article dated 1947 that said, "All Saints Church burial lands flooded;" another dated 1922 commemorated a town fire.

The Inn deserved its place as a landmark. Built in 1540 of oak timers and wattle clay walls the year Henry married Anne of Cleves and divorced her and married Catherine Howard, it was known as the Ballingdon Bull, and was the most picturesque building in Sudbury. Thirteen years later, in 1553, Sudbury obtained its first charter. From 1559 onward, it returned two members to Parliament and flourished from the cloth trade, with Clare, Lavenham, Hadleigh, and Long Melford. The Bull prospered with its town and received recognition for bull-baiting in its yard. Inn bull baiting was not only amusement, but also deemed a sanitary necessity for the preparation of meat. From the overseer of the Sudbury flesh market came the announcement to that effect: to "p'sent all such p'sons as shall, kill, or allow to be killed, or offer to selle any bulls flesh which hath not before been well and sufficiently bayted according to the aunciente orders, decrees, and customs of this Kingdom . . ."

Bull baiting eventually was recognized as cruel sport. Macauley maintained it was first suppressed, not because it gave great pain, but provided spectators pleasure. By early Georgian times, people who enjoyed it were a minority and it was not to the Inn's credit to have it continued because it became known as a place of bull baiters, cockfighters, gamesters, gamblers, card-sharpers, dice throwers, heavy smokers and drinkers. A 450 year-old building . . . and I slept in its solidity with its uneven walls and roofs, pink walls, archway, and pine doors with leaded panes. While we chatted with Mrs. White in the sitting room with its brick chimney breast and champfered beams (smoothed edges, semi-design), she said their bedroom has a mezzanine where the chimney curves. In the old days, servant girls would sleep up there on pallets of straw. She also explained why we saw so much pink in buildings in Suffolk. The juice of sloe is added to plaster which produces Suffolk pink; however, in the Stour valley, it is called Constable pink.

## Sudbury
## Mill Hotel

The Mill Hotel in Sudbury served tea according custom. Memorable due to its environment, like the tea room in Caley Mills, it originated as a mill, but with mechanization had become "derelict." Its renovation as a hotel-restaurant-tea room created a unique atmosphere. Surrounded by mill paraphernalia, a date on glass enclosed the enormous mill wheel at the entrance: "Suffolk 1889." Like the conditioned responses of Pavlov's dogs, I react automatically to the old 19th-century mills with recalling George Eliot's *The Mill on the Floss*. Old mill stones stood watch at the hotel entrance. Perhaps the most interesting tale we encountered from legends and signs in East Anglia rests in the lobby corner of the hotel:

> "An age old East Anglian custom was that by burying a live cat in a building under construction, it would protect it from all harm by witches, warlocks, and fire. The mummified cat buried below was found in the timber framed part of this building during its conversion in 1971. It was obviously a victim of this superstition when the building was originally constructed nearly 300 years ago. It was re-interred on November 15, 1975, after four years eventful absence from the building."

We could only turn, look at each other, and wonder without speaking what "events" brought it "home." Was the Mill Hotel in need of "protection" again? What tales do lurk? Where did it spend the four years? Was it on vacation? What a lovely mystery!

# ⤝⟾ *Debenham* ⟾⤞
## *The Tawny Owl*

Another of the animal kingdom which enjoyed less than popular approbation was the owl. So, with interest, we noted that Debenham's listed tea room sported the name, The Tawny Owl. Because I navigated as the Sergeant Major Driver-ess negotiated the lanes, roads, and carriageways, I developed the custom of highlighting the map before we embarked so I could be more proficient in my duties. Whether we entered and exited correctly the curiously marked road signs was another matter, and if we did not always know where we were, we did know without hesitation where we were supposed to be.

Our journey to Debenham occurred when we traveled from Diss to Eye en route to Framlingham. Because our visit trip through Debenham came so early in the morning, we elected to return on another excursion two days later. En route, we passed Earl Sohan where there were men in costume dancing in front of the Victoria Pub, and we saw duck eggs advertised at a country lane gate for 78 pence a dozen ($1.23). A load of hay pulled onto the road in front of us just before we reached the Debenham sign. We slowed, and I glanced idly to the left where I noticed a strange mound and square cement with slits. Suddenly, a curious chill ran over me, and I sat up straight to look back when I realized it was a gun bunker, or maybe lookout from WWII.

At The Tawny Owl, we varied the tea food by testing a whole wheat roll and home made soup. The decor was pleasant: the customary dark wood ladder back chairs with tapestry seats; beamed ceiling and brick fireplace with a black hood coming down over all of it; rose and brown roses in the carpet; brown and white checked table cloth; and brown and white dishes. Debenham appeared to be a quiet village; the patrons seemed equally subdued. A forty-something couple by the window sat engrossed in their quiet conversation. A mother and father with a little girl in royal blue sweats, about ten, leaned toward each other with the parents speaking to the child as to an adult. Skilled eavesdropper that I am, I could not catch a phrase from anyone.

Then, it was back on A1120 to Earl Stonham. Norma commented, "We came through here. Are we turned around?" I announced with pride, my finger on the map, "That was Earl Soham." From Earl Stonham and Soham we progressed confidently to A140, then A45, and to A12 to "home" for the night. I did it all by myself. Correction. We did it all by ourselves. And we did not even need to remember Gresham Court.

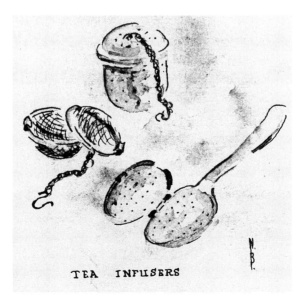

TEA INFUSERS

# X.
# Journey's End

As we met the Norfolk sign upon re-entry from Suffolk, we knew a sense of coming home. Though just five days since we had traveled there, ages seemed to have passed since we had been in Diss. We felt that we, like the buildings, should wear a date somewhere. And London! Well, I could scarcely remember it. That was seven days ago.

Full hours and multiple experiences, ticking in a fast march, one behind the other, have a way of vacuuming time and space, ballooning them out, making the capacity for even short distances and small segments seem larger than reality. So, GSL-Navigator-Archivist, mapped us back through East Anglia to the dual carriageway, A12, and London, past areas listed in Domesday with Danish domination. But we recognized all that had gone before us as the pummeling and positioning of life to make a loaf worthy of the flowers that grace the table where service is given.

In the time since that conversation with Mr. Dell Brower when I said I had never tried to trace my ancestors, I have recalled family stories of my Grandfather Sherman's tales of General William Tecumseh Sherman's march through Georgia and Alabama: Sherman that he was. And I have seen pictures of the General and can recognize some facial similarities. But I also know there is Indian ancestry in the background of both my paternal grandparents, and I weave tales about that, too. In reverie, I sometimes wonder why I, enamored of individual stories in grave yards, have so little interest in my own genealogy. I think it must be that I am, at heart, more Puritan American than family-fixed regionalist. Those cultural ancestors emigrated from East Anglia as furious democrats (note the small *d*), intent on leaving the trappings of aristocracy to make a land of their choosing. As historian Daniel Boorstin notes, America became a land where, through the centuries, strangers on a first name basis have come together to create community. That kind of radical individualism interests me far more than family bloodlines; that fascination draws me to grave yards to ponder what might have been in the lives of the lonely sleepers where family matters little in the solitary evidence for their having lived. I have no preoccupation with ancestral exploits. The time required to learn such would rob me of some investment in my own pursuits. Interesting as Dell Brower's information was about Thomas Sherman's house, I prefer to traipse around East Anglia visiting tea rooms and geography which have produced both history and aesthetic expansions rather than to look for family connections. Whoever they were, they produced me, and I would thank them if I could, for I find eminent joy in my life, so I will honor them by making the most of their creation.

"On the road again," we turned toward London and Harley House. The Sergeant Major Vicar's Wife and "The Keep" brought GS Lewis Navigator-Archivist straight to Pete and JoAnn Jennings and a hot cooked meal. No tea. No midnight journaling. Instead we indulged in hot decaffeinated coffee and a wonderful TV movie, *Shadowland*, the story of C.S. Lewis and his Joy. My thoughts turned homeward to W.C. Lewis, my joy, the ultimate loaf and hyacinth of my life.

*East Anglia Windmill*

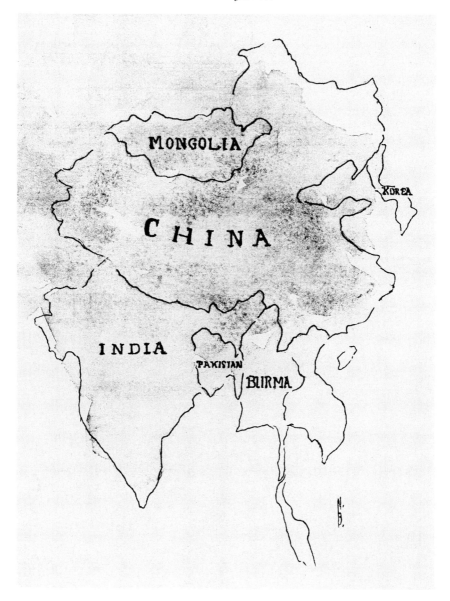

# AFTERWORD
## ⇢⟨⟩═ *A Buffet of Other Loaves* ═⟨⟩⇠

### *Loaf 1: History of Tea*

The Chinese used tea as early as the 28th century B.C. While the earliest Trojan culture rooted and the first terraced tower temples in Mesopotamia soared, tea brewing occurred in the Orient. Emperor Chinnung collected agricultural and medicinal knowledge of tea in the mid-2700s B.C. while Cheops, or Khufu, Pharaoh of the Fourth Eyptian Dynasty, built the Great Pyramid at Giza and the Sphinx nearby with its face as his portrait.

During the tenth century B.C., the Chinese kept written records of tea when David was King of Israel, the Phoenicians ascended in sea power, and the Ionians, dispossessed in Greece, formed the first Ionian Confederacy in Asia Minor. With all the Chinese poetry written prior to 550 B.C., a book of poems edited by Confucius mentioned tea.

Early tea use is shrouded in mysticism with tales of its being taken by holy men to remain alert in their meditation. Legends survive with their supernatural explanations of tea's origin. One story tells of the Indian founder of Ch'an Buddhism who prayed before a wall for years without rest. One day, he fell asleep. Grieved by his slip from devotion, he cut away his eyelids and threw them on the ground. Without a stop, five years of meditation followed. When he felt sleepy again, he noticed a shrub where he had flung his eyelids. Chewing its leaves, he was refreshed and continued his spiritual vigil.

Buddhist monks took tea to Japan in 794 A.D., the year Norsemen landed in Ireland and Byzantine Empress Irene overthrew and blinded her son, Constantine. Tea held religious significance for the Ch'an Buddhists, precursors of Zen Buddhists in Japan. Zen tea procedures formed the basis for *Cha-no-yu*, meaning "the way of tea," the centuries-old Japanese tea ceremony. In its modified form, the ritual is still a part of Japanese cultural life.

The Japanese were growing tea all over their country in the 800s when Norsemen invaded Germany, Pope Leo II crowned Charlemagne the Holy Roman Emperor, and the Incas built their sacred city, *Machu Pichu*, in Peru.

In China, Lu Yu, sometimes called Lo Yu, wrote his historical narrative, *Tea Classic (Ch'a Ching)* in 780. The tenor of his manuscript is a combination of Madison Avenue hardsell and Western USA frontier medicine show hype. It reveals the Chinese obsession with tea together with extravagant claims for its use. By the eighth century, Chinese tea use became so common that its consumption was taxed.

A year after Kublai Khan died, Marco Polo returned from China in 1295, the year "The Harrowing of Hell," an early miracle play, was appearing in English hamlets. In 1298, he started his memoirs in a Genoese jail. Although he elaborated on the riches and splendor of Oriental life, he never mentioned tea. Europe's first written account of *ch'a*, as it was called in Canton, or *te*, in Amoy dialect, came in 1559. The year Robert, Lord Dudly, became the favorite of Elizabeth I, Giovanni Battista Ramusio, a Venetian nobleman, wrote a travel tales book called *Delle Navigationi et Viaggi*. The author described Chinese tea customs and rivaled Lu Yu in his exhorbitant testimonials to tea's effects.

Oriental trade in silks and spices came to Europe first by overland Persian caravans to Venetian merchants. Late in the fifteenth century, the Spanish and Portuguese exploded world trade balance with long range sailing ships and ocean current maps. Vasco de Gama rounded the Cape of Good Hope to find a route to India, and ocean lanes became the source for eastern trade. In the first five years of the 1500s, Lucretia Borgia married the Duke of Ferrara; Canterbury Cathedral was finished; Michelangelo freed "David" from stone; Henry, Prince of Wales, denounced his marriage to Catherine of Aragon; book printing proliferated; and the pocket handkerchief came into use. In 1506, Jokob Fugger, an Augsberg merchant, imported spices from the East Indies to Europe by sea the first time.

During the sixteenth century, Spain and Portugal controlled Eastern trade, albeit with dependency on Spain's rule of the Dutch, their gold, and powerful merchants. Though direct trade with Western Europe flourished, tea appeared in Europe first in Russia in 1567. Jars of it were imported to Moscow by 1638, and in 1689, by Chinese treaty, tea caravans began to cross Siberia. Russians developed the samovar for their distinctive tea customs, whereby tea was constantly ready in a household, brewed in a small pot on top of a larger urn holding hot water for dilution.

Holland declared its independence from Spain in 1581, the year Elizabeth I knighted Francis Drake and the folk song, "Greensleeves," appeared in written records. In 1588, the Vatican Library began, Marlowe's *Doctor Fautus* appeared, and England defeated the Spanish Armada. With Spanish sea power broken, the Dutch and English developed a monopoly of Eastern trade. Holland dominated first, with its Dutch East India Company that established trading posts in Asia and Africa. A Dutch seaman's travelogue itemized the steps of the Japanese tea ceremonies and practices in 1595, the same year the English Army abandoned the bow as a weapon, heels became a part of shoes, and Shakespeare wrote *Richard II*.

Early in the seventeenth century, the Dutch secured Bantam, near Java, for trade. Chinese junks waddled there with their tea cargoes. Tea was first sent to Europe directly from Bantam in 1606, the year Galileo perfected his proportional compass and Guy Fawkes was sentenced to death. Initially, tea was used as filler for vacant shipping space, but within thirty years, the Dutch East India Company was dealing in large amounts of tea for profit. Dr. Cornelius Decker wrote *Diatribe on Fevers*, a book of the ilk of those written by Lu Yu and Ramusio, claiming tea's universal virtues. He advocated excessive tea consumption, in the vein of some contemporary claims for vitamin ingestion. His avowal that he drank 200 cups a day was dismissed, however, with the discovery that the Dutch East India Company was his employer. A Mr. Wickham, an agent of the British East India Company, was the first Englishman to mention tea. He wrote from Firando, Japan, June 27, 1615, to Mr. Eaton, a company officer in Macao, requesting "a best pot of the best sort of chaw." Mr. Eaton's accounts reflected, additionally, "three silver porringers to drink chaw in."

The English, celebrated tea drinkers of the world, came late to the custom. Coffee and ale were the British drinks until the later 1600s. In 1650, the same year that Harvard College in the New World was granted a charter, the first coffeehouse opened in Oxford, England. The establishments quickly spread, and London was soon filled with them. Coffeehouses satisfied a public need in day-to-day business and social life as places of the literati, economic transactions, political dialogue, news exchange, intrigue alliance, and early postal development. With Cromwell taking over the government, some considered them sedition nests.

Due to cost, tea was first the aristocracy's drink, but with massive imports, prices fell, and tea drinking spread across Europe. Through Europe, tea came to England in scanty quantities, and its cost was prohibitive to all but the wealthy. However, in 1658, Thomas Garaway, a London coffeehouse owner, became the first English tea dealer with an advertisement that tea would be offered in his business. The same announcement ran in two publications:

> That excellent and by all Physitians approved China drink called by the Chineans Tcha, by other nations Tay, alias Tee, is sold at the Sultaness Head, a chopheeshouse, in Sweetings Rents, by the Royal Exchange, London. *The London Gazette* (No. 432, September 2-8, 1658) and *Mercurius Politicus* (No. 435, September 23-30, 1658)

Others related their experiences with tea and history. Samuel Pepys, England's eminent diarist who was an eye-witness to the execution of Charles I and in the fleet which brought Charles II from exile, wrote on September 25, 1660, "I did send for a cup of tea, a China drink of which I never had drunk before."

Charles II was crowned in 1661. The next year he married the Infanta Catherine of Braganza, a tea-drinking Portuguese princess, who replaced ale with tea at court functions. In 1664, the British East India Company gave the king two pounds and two ounces of tea. Two years later, the king's tea gift weighed twenty-two and three-quarters pounds.

Britain's relationship with tea became more complex. In the mid-1670s, a petition presented to the government requested prohibition of tea, stating it interfered with the consumption of barley, malt, and other native products. Coffee did not escape criticism. "The Women's Petition Against Coffee" alleged that the drink made men "unfruitful as the deserts when the unhappy berry is brought," and called the drink "ninnybroth" and "turkey-gruel." To recover revenues lost from the alcohol tax because people were drinking tea, Charles did initiate a tax, a reminder that protective trade laws are not a new concept. Neither is lobbying a recent practice. In February, 1684, the British East India Company directors wrote to Madras, "In regard thea is grown to be a commodity here, and we have occasion to make presents therein to our great friends at court, we would have you send us yearly five or six cannisters of the very best and freshest thea." Tea eventually accomplished the Spanish Armada's failed task; it conquered England.

British traders decided to compete with the Dutch for the lucrative tea market. Both companies maintained warships and armies. The ensuing struggle was deadly, culminating with the British dominating in India and China, and the Dutch controlling Indonesia, the Malay peninsula, and Japan. By the close of the seventeenth century, the British East India Company was importing 20,000 pounds of tea a year. In 1703, the annual amount was 105,000 pounds. By the end of the eighteenth century, tea consumption in Britain averaged two pounds a person per year and continued to rise over the next hundred years. In the 1980s, as the world's top tea consumer, England imported 200,000 metric tons a year. At the rate of one cup a day, one pound yields almost a year's supply. In second place, the USA imported 80,000 metric tons annually. The Dutch ranked third, with 40,000 metric tons as their yearly quota.

Tea's great challenger in the eighteenth and nineteenth centuries was alcohol, not coffee. Eventually, it bowed to beer in Germany and to the great wines in France. Although ale was a daily drink of adults and children in England, tea fused with the national consciousness, once its use was established. Queen Anne, who gave royal approval to the sweepstakes idea, began serving tea at court breakfasts in 1702, the year of the first pantomime in Dury Lane and the French New World settlement in what is now Alabama. As the British learned to brew tea, they made it at home, and it became their breakfast drink.

In the early 1840s, British difficulties with China necessitated an independent source for tea. Entrenched in India, the British East India Company discovered an indigenous tea in Assam, a northeast state, and began British cultivation. Commercial growing spread to Formosa, now Taiwan, and Ceylon, now Sri Lanka. Growing expanded in other ways: Russians developed their industry in the Caucasus; independently, Natal started the crop.

Tea-drinking enjoyed a sociological turn when Anna, Seventh Duchess of Bedford, initiated afternoon tea time in 1840, the year Queen Victoria married Prince Albert, Pierre Auguste Renoir was born, Napoleon's ashes were placed in the Invalides, and James Fenimore Cooper's *Pathfinder* was a best seller. The Duchess did not burst on the scene with a revolutionary idea for a British institution. Taking tea had evolved in the daily food cycle rhythm in relation to the main meal. The wealthy ate their largest meal late in the evening, so a small repast with tea was taken at 6 p.m. to nourish them until the dinner hour. Laboring classes had their principal meal at noon, so their "high" or "meat" tea was taken with noon leftovers as supper. Anna's tea occurred earlier in the afternoon, at 4 p.m., the hour currently considered tea-time.

Settlers in America drank coffee first. The Mayflower had a coffee grinder on board, and English colonists did not develop a taste for tea until the early 1700s. However, in New Amsterdam, tea was more common than in London, since the Dutch shipped it there as early as 1626. When the settlement became New York, tea gardens remained popular places for society. Tea assumed an ominous symbolism for the colonials with the Stamp Act of 1765, legislation designed to defray costs of the French and Indian War. Violent protest caused its repeal, but a new tax was passed in 1767. The colonials boycotted the British Company, but did not forego their tea; Dutch smugglers supplied their needs. In 1770, Parliament repealed the Townshend Acts that taxed imports to the colonies, but retained the tea duty to show authority. Three British ships arrived at Boston harbor in November, 1773, with 342 chests of tea. Boston citizens did not permit unloading and the royal governor would not allow the tea clippers to leave until the tax was paid. On December 16, 1773, the Sons of Liberty boarded the ships and threw the tea into the harbor. Interestingly, one of the first acts of the new post-Revolution federal government, when direct tea trade started, was to tax tea five to fifteen time higher (depending on the tea quality) than the British tax. Tea never overcame the economic disadvantage, and its consumption has always ranked after coffee in North America.

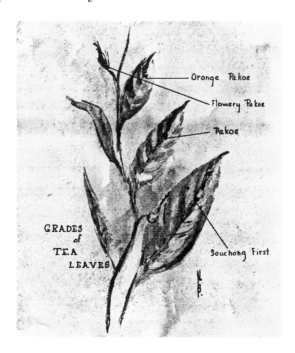

## *Loaf 2: Tea Plant and Production*

The natural habitat of the tea plant is a fan-shaped area which extends from Assam and Darjeeling in northeast India to Chekiang in China, and south through Burma and Thailand into Vietnam. The three main varieties of the plant are most distinctive in the extremes of the area, bearing the names of the places where they are grown: China, Assam, and Cambodia. The latter serves primarily for crossing with other varieties. Having a wide range of adaptability, the tea plant is cultivated in China, Japan, India, Pakistan, Sri Lanka, Taiwan, Indonesia, Russia, Malaysia, and African nations in the area of Kenya. Other countries produce tea without entering the world market.

Nor do they grant exotic names to the product.

The tea plant, *Camellia sinensis*, is an evergreen of the family *Theaceae*. It grows fifteen to thirty feet tall in its natural state, but when cultivated and restricted by plucking and pruning, it remains a bush, two to five feet in height. Its spearhead-shaped serrated leaves grow on short stalks which average one-and-a-half to ten inches long and one-half to four inches wide. The axils of the leaves hold fragrant flowers, either singly or in groups of two to three. Each flower has five white petals encompassing bright yellow stamens. The highest quality tea comes from the **pekoe tip** or **flowery pekoe**. The **orange pekoe** leaf is next to the leaf bud. Following down the shoot is the **pekoe** leaf, then **first souchang**, **second souchang**, **first congou**, and **second congou**. Usually, only the first three kinds of leaves are harvested.

A tea plant is harvested every forty days, or when there is a new **flush**, a full complement of leaves. A four-step process prepares the leaves for production of black tea. They are wilted to allow fermentation to start. After wilting, rolling spreads juices on the leaves. Then they are spread to ferment, or oxidize, two to four hours, or the length of time indicated for the particular leaves. Last, firing stops the fermentation and prevents rotting. Leaves for green tea follow three phases: steaming, rolling, and firing. Oolong tea, which is more robust than green tea but milder than black, proceeds through the stages of black tea, but is not fermented as long.

Tea is graded for style, a term encompassing the age and size of the leaf. Tea tasters grade the quality. Traders buy teas at auction to blend and package for individual markets. Bids are made according to information provided by tea tasters who judge a tea by its dry leaf, infused leaf, and the infusion proper. The tea taster's vocabulary has 120 terms.

Unblended black teas are Assam, Ceylon, Ching Wo, Darjeeling, Flowery Orange Pekoe, Keemun Congou, Kenya, Lapson Souchong, Orange Pekoe, Russian, and Yunnan. Unblended ooolong teas have the names Black Dragon, Formosa Oolong, and Mainland Oolong. Unblended green teas are called Chun Mee, Dragon Well, Gunpowder, Gyokuru, Pingsuey, Young Hyson, and Yunnan Tipped. Many variations arise as possibilities for blended teas, depending on the area where they are grown, their grade, and their name. The traditional blended teas are Chinese Restaurant, Dragon-moon, English Breakfast, French Blend, Irish Breakfast, Lady Londonderry, Prince of Wales, Earl Grey, Queen Mary Blend, Russian Blend, and Russian Caravan.

## *Loaf 3: Tea Preparation*

When brewed, tea produces a liquor with caffeine, tannin, and aroma. In antiquity, it was made by boiling the leaves. Pottery teapots for infusion date to the sixteenth century in China. They have changed little since their beginning, with most variations being in a search for a composition that could withstand heat.

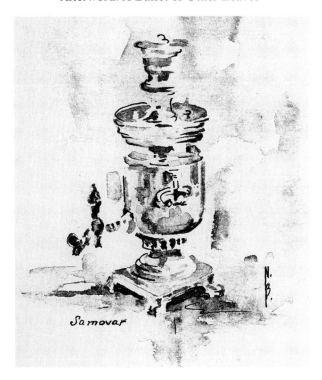

Samovar

With the growth of tea manufacturing, teaware production became an adjunctive industry. Josiah Wedgewood's lovely pottery and Josiah Spode's exquisite bone china of the eighteenth century vied with the silver teapots of the seventeenth century in beauty. When molds for ceramic pots could be made, unlimited teaware ornamentation came into vogue. Tea services became popular. Groups of vessels for making and serving tea were designed as sets. Pots, cream jugs, tea caddies, sugar bowls, tongs, tea spoons, strainers, cups and saucers, on a matching tray, provided aesthetic enjoyment for the physical pleasure of taking tea.

Mechanical gadgetry came with the nineteenth century and its emphasis on science and invention. People could boil eggs while heating tea water and press leaves on the pot's bottom. The tea ball infuser appeared; an American patented a timer; an Englishman invented an electric pot. Individual ideas shaped the tea practice. Iced tea is an American drink, but it originated with an Englishman. Richard Bleckendyn poured his tea over ice at the St. Louis World Fair in 1904 when he could not sell it because of the hot weather. Thomas Sullivan, a New York wholesaler, sent tea samples in small silk bags instead of the usual tins to his customers. Filter paper bags of the current market are the result. Produced first in the 1940s, instant teas have now progressed to being flavored, water soluble in cold water, and caffeine-free.

Teacups were small bowls at first. Oriental ones still do not have handles, and have different uses, dictated by their designs. Handled cups were in Europe when tea arrived. Russians and Middle East-erners use tea glasses. Saucers appeared in the early 1800s as hold-ers for the hot liquid.

## *Loaf 4: Tea Taster*

During our flight to London, I read in a one-page article in an airline magazine about a Mr. Peter Reddyhoff of Jackson Teas, London, a professional tea taster. Intrigued with the information and the apparent charm of the gentleman, even in print, I determined to try to find him and request an interview for our purposes.

Our first stop was Piccadilly Circus to visit a tourist centre and bank. We walked about Piccadilly Circus after returning via the tube, looking for several things, one being Jackson's Teas of Piccadilly and Mr. Peter Reddyhoff, their taster, without success. The proprietor at the china shop where I ordered a tea warmer said Jackson's had left

Piccadilly. Later, we discovered where they moved, and I tried to get in touch to make an appointment for a time when we returned from our road trips. From the Jennings flat, I called the number and noted the address in the telephone book, 01-228-2332, 66 St. John's Road, different from the information in the article. Our hopes were up that we might be able to see him sooner than anticipated since the area was not far from Harley House. When I dialed, nothing happened.

Again.

Nothing.

"I'm not getting through," I said to Norma, "Do I dial direct?"

Norma, "Try the operator."

We discovered how to dial the operator—not 0.

Male voice. "Yasss."

"I'm dialing 228-2332 and do not get it to ring. Is it a working number?"

"What is youah numbah, plisss?"

I told him.

"I shall have to check it if you'd like."

"Yes. Please."

Silence.

"Yasss. That numbah is unattainable."

"I beg your pardon."

"That numbah is unattainable."

"Do you mean it isn't working or that the party no longer has it?"

"Well, I shall have to make inquiries. I can call you later."

"My problem is that I am leaving town and won't be here for your answer."

"In that case, I shall check for you straightaway. Hold, plisss."

Silence.

"Hallo. That number has been changed to 669-4494." (Only he said "Double 69-double 494," which I had to have repeated twice.)

"That's Jackson's Teas of Piccadilly?"

"Right! Shall I ring for you?"

"Please. Thank you."

Ringing. (Two rings and a wait).

"Helloo." Female voice.

"May I speak with Mr. Peter Reddyhoff, please?"

"Mr. Reddyhoff is on holiday."

"I see. Could you tell me your address, please?"

"190 London Road. Hackbridge. Wallington Surrey. Postal number SM67EX." (That information was gained with much repetition and question and answers like S-Samuel, M-Mother.)

"May I leave a message for Mr. Reddyhoff, please? I'm leaving London for two weeks, but would like to speak with him when I return."

"Actually, he's just on our premises."

"Isn't this Jackson's Teas?"

"No."

"Is the address you just gave me yours, or theirs?"

"Ours. But they're on our premises. Would you like to speak with one of Mr. Reddyhoff's associates? Would you like me to ring them?"

"Yes. Please."

Ringing.

"Hello!" Chipper, male voice.

"I am calling for Mr. Peter Reddyhoff."

"He's away on holiday."

"My name is Gladys Lewis and I was hoping to speak with him on the basis of a magazine article I read of an interview with him. May I leave my name?"

"Yes. Of course!"

"I'm leaving London for a couple of weeks, but I will call him when I return."

"Sure. Of course."

I spelled my name, and was bade a cheery goodbye. I felt a sense of victory, even knowing I might never find him again.

Because we moved between several towns in an outing, the day in Cambridge presented the best opportunity to attempt a call, since we intended to be in town all day. I had five 50p coins ready when I rang the operator and told her what I wanted.

"You wish to reverse the charges?"

"No."

"Why don't you dial direct?"

"I want to make a person-to-person call. He might not be in."

"You'll have to deposit coins."

"I know."

"Your name?"

"Gladys Lewis."

"Number."

I told her the number on the phone box.

Long wait.

"The number is inaccessible. We'll ring you back in ten minutes.

Hang up. Long wait. Phone rang.

"Yes?"

"Deposit one pound fifty pence."

My coin slot would not open. The process required two operators to get it to open. I deposited.

"Now, one pound forty for the call."

"I just did deposit."

"But this is for the call."

"I don't have any more coins. Can you return what I've deposited and I'll get more change, then return?"

"Sorry. The coins are already registered in the box. Dial 198 when you return."

I hurried away. No store would give me change. Finally, I went into a chemist's and bought a 30 pence roll of candy with a ten pound note, but the girl would only give me three 50 p. coins. So I bought another one, with another paper note, on the opposite cashier.

Back to the phone, just in time. A "queue" began to form as I closed the door. I dialed 198, explained my story to two people, and got back to the call.

"Your number is unattainable (busy). We'll try again."

I waited, trying not to look at the people outside the phone box and attempting to appear British, not American. Finally, the phone rang.

"You may go ahead. Deposit one pound forty."

"Will one pound fifty be all right?"

"Yes."

I shoved them in.

"Deposit one 50 p coin more."

"I did."

"Look in the exchange plate. It didn't register."

I picked up the errant coin and shoved it in the box.

"Hello." A cheery, exuberant, male, British voice.

"Hello, Mr. Reddyhoff ! " I explained that I'd left my name earlier, was returning to London, and would like an appointment for an interview.

"Now what was the nature of the interview?"

I explained.

"Tuesday?"

"Yes."

"I think I'll be gone all that day. I'm checking. Yes."

"I am so sorry."

"When will you be back in London?"

"The following Monday."

"I can see you then."

"Wonderful! What time shall I come?"

"Three o'clock Monday afternoon, the 12th."

I WAS SO HAPPY. I fairly skipped from the phone boxes, praying to any divine source attuned to me that I could conduct a good interview, but my confidence was soaring from having found him with my tracking and negotiating the obstacles.

Back in London, we continued our search for the mystical Mr. Peter Reddyhoff. We had to take a train to Hackbridge and after a hike past Brooke Bond's warehouse to Parrish and Fen, we finally met Mr. Peter Reddyhof. And he was worth the search. Norma, with her art, and I, with my words, could not have created a more perfect specimen of the British gentleman. He was tall, fair, impeccably groomed, and so charming he made my teeth hurt. Readily, he gave permission for me to tape the conversation and relaxed at his desk with the two of us flanking him.

I began my questions. What does your position with Jackson's involve?

"It has to do with marketing, that is getting the right product to the right place with the right prices at the right time, looking at market trends. We try to see how we can use the expertise that we have to fill those market trends."

"You told us of your trips abroad in the interests of your work. You mentioned some places you've gone in the US."

"I travel the whole US with our importers, with their salesmen and brokers, right across the country to those parts that use tea. You've got part of the west coast, practically the whole of the east coast, some of the midwest and probably the rest of the US never even heard of tea." (Laughter)

"Could you give us an overview of a tea company's work? What is involved with choice of teas to import? What is the process from the beginning?"

"Basically, a tea company blends teas. A friend of mine who is in India works for a company that owns about 45 estates in India and travels the world selling his company's teas. We call those teas originals because they come from the estates where they are grown. His company's teas are called original teas. The thing that is said more to him than anything else is, 'Ah, yes, but the best teas are grown in England.' Now basically, that's because we've got the art of blending. Now blending is like an artist mixing color. We want a particular color and a particular taste. Many people try to blend teas by computer, and it doesn't work. Tea is a living substance. It is grown year on year and on the same estate. The same tea will change. If you taste it two months after it's grown, then taste it four months after its grown, and when you are picking, it will have a completely different character, because the weather's changed and all sorts of things may have happened. The taste is completely different from year to year. Therefore, a tea blender's going to have all this knowledge in his mind and on his palette. He's going to mix tea, and he's going to get the same taste, the same color, the same leaf size as he did on the last blend. And that's the art of the blender."

"Is there a preparation or a specified training for a tea taster?"

"Oh, yes. You can be taught to taste tea, but you can't be taught to value tea. That's something you have instinctively. You can taste tea. In half an hour, I can get you tasting tea, and you recognize an Assam or a Darjeeling, but you wouldn't recognize all the gardens within that. For instance, with over 3 thousand different tea marks in China, which is a tea name, a good tea blender will know most of those. He'll know the taste, he'll know the color, he'll be able to recognize them. Then you add to that all the Indian teas, all the African teas, and all the South American teas. As you can see, it takes years and years to perfect the art."

"But there aren't that many good tasters in the entire world. I can tell you different gardens, but I couldn't tell you all the gardens. But what we basically do is buy teas . . . we have a certain standard that we want to achieve both in color and in leaf and in appearance. We buy teas which come from the various auctions in London, Colombo, Calcutta, and Amsterdam. We buy from all those four auctions. At the same time, we buy direct from the estates from the country of origin. Based on the price that we want to receive and the cost we want to get, when all the teas arrive, we start to blend them, which is basically just mixing teas together to get the same taste and the same color we've always had. You then get a blender who can produce something which, to all intents and purposes, is exactly the same as the last blend. If you look at the teas in that blend, and look at the teas in the last blend, there's not one that's the same. I've actually had an Assam blend without a single pound of Assam tea in it. I've taken it to India, and they didn't even know the difference. That's blending. That's perfect blending."

"Fascinating."

"Absolutely. You see, if you buy originals—and in America, you sell a lot of original teas—you buy garden marks and sell them as a Darjeeling or an Assam or something else. The problem with that is there is only so much that is ground at a time, and the next time you pick that tea, it may have changed, so you can't follow it. The taste, color, everything, is different . . . and the price is most certainly different. We blend to keep the quality, the color, everything, the same. So you look at all the blend sheets that you write down. One time you may be doing a blend of Earl Grey and you've got about ten different teas. The next you may even have fifteen, or you may only have seven."

"How many times would you blend? How many harvests a year?"

"Oh, well, there it depends on the country. In India . . . I'm taking north India, south India, and Darjeeling . . . the average length of time you are picking is about seven months. In Africa, you can pick eleven months because of different climactic conditions. We are blending everyday . . . not all the same blends, but we are blending continuously day in and day out."

"Your company is the oldest, I believe, of the London tea companies?"

"Debatable. It is one of the oldest. If you go back to 1604, there were Jackson's in the Piccadilly area, as there were Twinings and Ridgeways round about the same sort of age. I think we are just about the oldest. There aren't that many of us at that age."

"What precipitated the move from Piccadilly's? We traced you through the telephone company to find you."

"Oh, that's a long history. Our tea company as such has never actually been in Piccadilly . . . the company of Jackson's of Piccadilly. When I joined Jackson's about fifteen years ago, we had 24 shops, grocery shops, in various places, Fortnum & Mason's, Harrad's, others, but selling nothing but food. Over a long period of time, business has changed in this country, as it has in America and the rest of the world. Supermarkets have come in. Even the royal family go to supermarkets now to do their shopping. They used to come to Jackson's. They still come for incidentals. But general food requirements are bought in supermarkets. And what we have found is the style of business has changed. If you take our Tunbridge Wells Shop, for instance—a lovely old town, lovely old spar town–all the huge houses around our shop are all now offices. So all the people have moved away from the shops. In our Piccadilly store, which is the last one we closed . . . five years ago . . . we had 69 staff. Now you can't sell food in central London and have 69 staff. The staff would take just as much care selling you a pound of bacon as they would selling you ten pounds of caviar. And you can't get that type of staff anymore. We found that the four years of our lease was up and the new rent was going to be about 150,000 pounds a year. That's just the rent. There's no way you can sell enough food . . . not with the mark-ups on food . . . because food mark-up margins in this country are very much smaller than they are in America–very much smaller. Tea in this country, for instance, starts at about 9 percent up to about 16 percent. Sometimes it is sold at a loss. Assam tea starts at 25 percent, but even at that price, you can't make money and pay the rent. The whole business has changed. So we have actually sold our shops and concentrated on investing in our tea company. And that's why you find us here. The reason why we are in these offices is because last June we sold our company to a public company. The firm who normally lives here, Parish and Finn, are our distributors in the UK and since we were that close together in terms of business anyway, we thought we might move and get even closer together, and that's why we are here. So Jackson's are alive and well and living in Hackbridge." (Laughter)

"Yes. And we found you!"

"You found us! Good detective work."

Norma asked, "Was tea cultivated in Scotland at one time?"

"No. Not that I know of."

"I thought I had read somewhere it had been. I knew that climactic conditions would not be right. But when Ceylon companies had problems, I thought I heard about their giving it a try in Scotland and it working for awhile but I could not imagine that."

"Never heard of it. (Laughter) It was grown in America."

"What part?"

"Alabama."

"When would that have been?"

"Not very long ago. About a hundred years ago."

"Did it work?"

"I don't know. "

"I never heard of it."

"They made more money out of cotton."

"True."

"The strange thing is that we have climactic conditions here very similar to Darjeeling. I brought back cuttings from Darjeeling completely legally. I can't grow them over here. Why, I don't know. There is one tea bush in England, and that is in Kew Gardens. Tea tree. They let it grow. See, the tea bush that we know is usually pruned to about four feet in height so the girls can pick. If you let it grow, it normally becomes a tree, 30-40 feet high. It's a magnificent tree. Looks like a large privet hedge. Do you know what privet is?"

"Yes."

"Lovely, oily green color, lovely, deep, rich green."

"We have a special interest in tea rooms and associate that with the custom of taking tea. What is your impression of an ideal situation for taking tea in the afternoon. Do you think it does have a more aesthetic quality taken in certain places or circumstances more than others?"

"It's like anything, isn't it? You can have a food, a drink, or you can do something. In the right surroundings, the activity always seems more enjoyable. Go to Joe's Café for a pot of tea, or a cup of tea, and go to the Ritz, say, and have exactly the same tea in the Ritz. Which one would you enjoy?"

"The Ritz! We've done it. (Laughter) We loved it!"

"I think that is the best value for a meal anywhere in the world. Not just London. It's what, about 8 pounds?"

"Less than that."

"Six pounds, something like that? Wonderful. Absolutely fantastic. We repackaged all our English products recently, and we launched them at the Ritz. We had a lunch first of all, and had the whole menu cooked with tea. In the afternoon, we had tea, the normal Ritz tea, and all the cakes were made with tea. We had orange flavored tea cake, we had lemon flavored tea cake–absolutely delicious. The whole thing was just superb. It's just the surroundings, pure and simply. But with the Ritz, it is something different. You do get money for money. It's like drinking a cup of tea out of a superb bone china teacup. It *tastes* better. It's like when you clean your car, your car seems to go better." (Laughter)

"Why do you think tea consumption caught on more quickly and has had a more lasting tenure with the British than with other countries when it was introduced in those places at about the same time? The British seem to have responded in a national way more than any other country we have encountered."

"I think if you go back in history, tea was very, very expensive when it first came into this country. It was something like 18 shillings 6 pence a pound which was worth in those days about 40-50 pounds now—wildly expensive. You need to look at the earning capacity of people in those days. The average Englishman couldn't afford to drink tea. It was just the very select few. And then, prior to the first world war, tea started getting cheaper. It became even cheaper, and during the war, it was rationed anyway. Tea is just something the British have taken to, whereas we've never really taken to coffee. The coffee business in this country is small. We drink more instant coffee than we do fresh coffee. You have better coffee in America. You have very good coffee in America if you go to the right places. But the average staff don't cater it here, and the coffee in hotels is simply appalling. It's tasteless; it's got nothing at all. And there again, they don't know how to make tea in America. You will get a tea bag and a jug of water which is not even hot, let alone boiling. You can't make a good cup of tea that way. I really don't know how to answer—probably something to do with the British. We like tea. And that's it. We drink gallons. The tea trade in this country is worth about five hundred million pounds sterling."

"Would you drink as much tea if you didn't work for Jackson's?"

"I always have drunk tea. You come to stages in life when you think about things. I can't drink teeth without sugar. I have a terribly sweet tooth, and I've got my habit down now to one spoon per cup. But one time, things were so bad, I started weighing out the amount of sugar I took in a day. It was astronomical. I decided I had to do something about it."

"And you take it with milk?"

"Oh, yes. There's no other way to take tea."

Reluctantly, we finished our interview with Mr. Reddyhoff and bade him goodbye, sharing on the return trip to London the feeling with the parting that we had gained a new friend.

## *Loaf 5: Tea Room Proprietors*
## *Sue and Terry Kilty of the The Bridge House Tea Rooms*

The Bridge House Tea Rooms sit on the bank of the Little Ouse River in Brandon. Charmed by Sue and Terry Kilty, the proprietors, we determined to return for a more extended conversation, upon her agreement to an interview. After settling ourselves, gaining permission for the taping, and turning on the recorder, we began with Sue.

"Your location is unique. Can you talk about the property and the setting for your tea rooms?"

"The house itself is about 250 years old. Originally, it was three watermen's cottages facing onto the river. The front was built in Victorian days using bricks which came from the original maltings which ran along the length of the garden. We know the age from the way of dating them. Even then, people did not use new bricks to rebuild. We've tried to keep the tradition up in building the cottage in old flint which has come from other cottages in the area, so we are also reusing materials on the site to try to keep it in harmony with its age and the type building that's been done around here."

"There were originally three cottages?"

"Yes. They were joined in Victorian times. The house was renovated to its present size in Victorian times. So the front that is now facing the road was originally the side of the houses and they were initially facing the river, with a set of three front doors."

"You mentioned that it is not often that houses like this come on the market. How did you find it and decide on moving here?"

"We actually found the house advertised in a magazine that I very much doubt you will have heard of. It is called the *Exchange in Marts*. It only carries classified advertising. Normally, it features secondhand cars, bits of old lorries, and the like. I mean, it's a glorified yard sale for the whole country, and for some reason the previous owner of this house thought it was the best place to put the sale notice. And we happened to have bought the magazine that week and saw the advertisement. We were coming up to East Anglia anyway, so we came to see the house and were amazed to find when he opened the front door that it was the same chap from whom we had bought our house in London . We never knew where he went. We learned that when we bought his house in London, he'd come up here and . . . we bought the house from him."

"Did Brandon have a special interest for you? Or did your interest in Brandon arise from the house?"

"We had never even heard of Brandon, which is a shame for it's a very historical village. In fact, its story stretches back to neolithic times. It's the site of man's oldest known trading with his neighbors. People exchanged the instruments that they made from flint for foodstuff which they couldn't grow readily in the area. So it's the first known example of capitalism, commerce."

"Flint, you have said, was very important for the economic growth of the area. Could you sketch that again about the economic ups and downs of the area?"

"Well, as man became more sophisticated, getting up to the fifteenth and sixteenth centuries, workers manufactured the flintlocks which went in the flintlock pistols. And there really wasn't a war fought anywhere in the world where the flintlocks didn't come from Brandon. But then, gunpowder was invented which wiped out the flint industry as far as Brandon was concerned, and they managed to pick themselves up by trading in rabbit furs, here in abundance, so they became the premier district for all tanning and cleaning of rabbit fur in the world. Pelts used to be sent here from Australia and New Zealand in the early days of the colonies for tanning, and in the leather lane district of London, there are still a lot of buildings called Brandon House, Brandon Street, and Brandon whatever. Then, a disease was introduced into the rabbits in this country to try and cull the numbers because they were becoming ridiculous. Unfortunately, it got into rabbits here and within a matter of months the whole colony of tens and tens and tens of thousands of rabbits were wiped out. Brandon didn't have a rabbit industry anymore. Then, the Americans came into the second World War not long after that. I think it was in the early '30s the rabbit industry was wiped out. Since then, there has been a huge American presence in the area and Brandon has learned to trade with the base and earn its living out of working directly or indirectly with the Americans on the base."

"We are sitting in your tea room, looking out, and seeing an American flag with the British flag, which is a warming sensation for us. We appreciate that on your part. You have many lovely antiques in your shop, and this is part of your business as well. Perhaps you could trace your interest in antiques and your special interest in restoring stained glass windows and having them here for sale."

"My interest in antiques goes back to being 16 and very, very broke. In those days in England, a lot of the furniture that you see around here was of a type that wasn't considered to be antique. It wasn't your actual Georgian, George III elbow chair, but rather, just ordinary, common old garden English Victorian furniture. That kind used to be very, very cheap to buy in this country. It was the cheapest way of furnishing a home. If you didn't mind that style of furniture, everybody was virtually throwing it out at the time. So I started furnishing a home like that, and it turned into a little sideline, because I kept buying pieces that I liked more than pieces I already had, and I would sell one piece and buy another. It was never a deliberate decision. Just over the years it built up into a huge collection. In fact, when we first opened the tea rooms, we didn't actually need to buy any tables and chairs. Other than the boats, we hardly bought a thing."

"Does your interest in restoring stained glass date to that time, or did that come later?"

"No. Terry's brother became interested in stained glass, and initially we started selling his glass, but then he decided that he didn't want us to sell it any longer, and by that time, we'd built up such a following that it seemed only logical to find our own glass and arrange to get it restored ourselves, and that's what we do now. It's become quite well-known that we always have glass here. A lot of the American tourists come up from London and English dealers come from all over the place. It's a very hard thing to find. There are very, very few shops in the country that actually sell stained glass. It's still very much a specialty market."

"How do you acquire your glass to restore?"

"Basically, you have to buy the glass either from the demolition men as they take buildings down, or from builders who are sometimes asked to take a particular window out if it's cracked, and replace it with another window. Sometimes I buy from glaziers, but I am always catching it in transit between the building and the rubbish skip. So, I started initially by passing my phone number around to everybody and anybody that I could think of that might have anything to do with a window coming out of a building somewhere. Eventually, some of those contacts bore fruit as people discovered that I was prepared to pay considerably more than the actual lead value of the window where they normally ended up in a scrap metal yard just for the lead value. Obviously the incentive was there for the builders to phone us rather sell the window for lead."

"You would acquire several a week, a month?"

"It's not like buying furniture, where you would go on a buying trip and say, 'I am going to buy a hundred tables.' Sometimes, somebody might phone me up and say, 'I have 9 or 10 windows if you are interested.' Then I might be scratching around another two months trying to buy some old windows. You can't *go* and buy them anywhere. They come to you."

"Mr. Kilty, would you repeat what you were saying about the toll keep."

"Hello. The bridge was originally built in the 1300s. In 1943, the Americans came along with a tank and knocked it down. When the GIs knocked the bridge down, they rebuilt it 'temporarily.' For about nine years, we had the wooden bridge. Eventually, the town council replaced it in 1954 with the present bridge. We have a gate in the garden where the road used to pass our house directly in front at that part . . . and see that apple tree there? The GI s during the war would come over the bridge in their tank, lean out their tank, and pick apples off the tree. Whilst they were doing that, they knocked the gate down. A big cast iron gate! Those GI s caused more damage in England than they did in Germany."

"I'm glad they finally did right by the bridge. You mentioned that the choice of decor was natural since you had a collection of antiques, Mrs. Kelty. What about your menu? Do you follow a set routine for the menu?"

"I was brought up a vegetarian. If you look closely at the menu, you will see that the only bit of meat on the menu is a ham sandwich. I am just happier cooking vegetarian dishes. We don't call ourselves vegetarian because that is very off-putting for a lot of people, but in fact a vegetarian diet is very suitable for a lunch-time restaurant. In any case, it is much lighter. The menu is based purely on personal preference, and I change it when I get fed up with cooking those particular things. We tear up the menus and start again."

"You do all of the cooking for the shop. How much time does that involve?"

"In the summer, we are up at half past six. We do bed-and-breakfast as well. So we make the breakfasts together, then generally Terry clears up and gets the restaurant ready for the day, and I start baking. I use the freezers very heavily. I freeze all my sponge cakes and scones and quiches and various breads. So each day, I cook for two or three hours one particular item on the menu, and freeze that, and use it in small quantities as we need it. Otherwise, I would have to cook maybe 24 different types of things each day, all at varying oven temperatures, which I just couldn't do. In the summer, we average about 200 people a day who are all eating a portion of something. That is quite a lot of food."

"Regarding clientele, do you have people who come regularly all the time, and do you have an increased number coming during the summer?"

"Yes, my regular customers are probably 90% American. But amongst all our customers, it probably is 65-70% because in the summer we have a very good passing trade of English people. The Norfolk hills is the place to have a traditional weekend cottage."

"The American tourists are staying away because of the international situation. We have not felt any anti-American feeling and feel safer in England in many regards than at home."

"I have not been aware of any anti-American feeling in this area. Perhaps some of the young lads in the village tend to resent the younger GIs taking out the 18 and 19-year-old girls because there aren't that many girls. And obviously, the young soldiers have far more money and are able to take them to all sorts of places. But this is the same in any garrison town. I don't think it makes any difference that they are American soldiers. I used to live in Windsor, and it had the same complaint because young soldiers are in full-time employment and a lot of the young lads just couldn't compete with them for the spending power. It would be a great shame if what has happened now continues and cause a hiccough in relations locally because there has not been any, and shouldn't be any because livelihood in the area lies directly or indirectly on the base. Ruining an economy is the most effective type of terrorism there is. Britain depends so heavily on its tourist economy now, which is largely American, that if that is killed, it will have detrimental effect on Anglo-American relations."

"How much renovation of the Bridge House was required?"

"We have completely and utterly restored the building. It had been lived in, although the chap we bought it from had only lived in it two years. The previous owners had been in the same family for 150 years and none of them had ever touched it. As far as we know, it dates back around 250 years. But it is not impossible in England for it to be that old or older, since there is no land registry. It would be very unlikely that there hadn't been a house on the site for longer since it was a ford crossing maybe four or five hundred years ago. Brandon was a site for stealing of saints remains between here and Durham. An elderly priest told us some of the stories. Was it Etheldreda? Of course, this would have been the crossing for any-one. People would stay somewhere overnight and cross in the morn-ing. This spot would be logical for accommodations."

"We read about that episode as we were driving up to Ely. We found the tale of Etheldreda fascinating. It is interesting that this is the place of her escape. I sense a great joy and fulfillment in your business here, Mr. Kilty."

"We came here from Brixton. It's like coming from Harlem to Paradise. That's why we like it so much here."

"How long have you had this location?"

"Five years."

"How long were you in Brixton?"

"Twenty-five years."

"Did you consider going further into East Anglia, Mrs. Kilty?"

"We were interested in being on the water. That was the main criteria. We looked at quite a number of properties. But most houses built on water in this country on river site have gone back through generations of family possession because water has always been important. So they tended to be the big, grand houses that were owned by the person who was most important, and he controlled the water. We had great difficulty finding any small houses on water, and

of course the large houses were out of our price range. They were
massive family homes, or they had long since been turned into hotels
and went for hundreds of thousands of pounds. This house is very,
very unusual in that it is still a small cottage because of the site of the
maltings. That is the original wall over there, the far side of the moor-
ings. And this is the other wall of it."

"Tell us about maltings."

"Maltings was where they malted the barley and other grains to
make beer. They had very long narrow buildings. This one stretched
to the other end of the garden. Our garage wall is constructed over
it. That one was definitely built before 1760. Those are the pre-
brick-tax bricks. And they have never been disturbed. They go
under water seven or eight feet. So we know that is the original wall.
We have paintings showing where the original maltings were standing. Because there was a huge, long dark building next to the garden, nobody wanted this little piece of land. Hence, it was the three
little cottages that were just workmen's cottages. They'd never, as
you would have expected, become the size of a grand home for
someone who could have afforded to live on the water."

"East Anglia is the most undeveloped part of Britain. There is no
moatway to London, no communication with the rest of the country.
That's why we still speak funny up here. The accent has remained up
here for much longer and it is much stronger. Very few people ever
came to East Anglia. It's pure Norfolk and Suffolk. So it is the fastest
growing region in the country now. The motorway comes to Barton
Mills now, just five miles down the road, and when it does eventually
come through here, as it will, everything will double in price then.
Brandon will be commutable to London then. And once you can get to
London, everything goes up. There is no other district in England so
close to London that is still so pure country. This area has been trans-

formed over the last ten years. We have an Australian lady staying here at the moment who lived here in '55, and she just cannot believe how much the area has changed. When she lived here, it was a village of 5000 population."

"How do you feel about the changes? Do you welcome it?"

"We have to welcome it because we are part of the change. We are part of the influx of outsiders that have come up here. It would be exceedingly hypocritical to say we don't like it. I suppose like most Londoners that come out of London, you want the country, but you dread that it's going to stay that way and obviously it must change."

"With being here, do you sense any disadvantages from being here with coming from London?"

"Night life. It's really an advantage. We neither earn as much money as we did in London, nor do we spend as much. We don't need as much."

"Do you have opportunities to get away together, or are you tied to the business year round?"

"We are tied. We went to great lengths last year to get all the paper work completed. We borrowed a house in Spain, got permission to take the vehicle to Spain, and arranged for people to come and stay here, so we could go to Spain. We got as far as Portsmouth docks, and we sat there and wondered what on earth we were doing. We turned around and we came home. We were away for exactly 24 hours. We stayed in somebody else's Bed-and -Breakfast for one night."

"How was the service?"

"Excellent! We came home with all sorts of ideas. That sounds awfully smug, but we enjoy it here. We are running the place that everybody else wants to come to. Where would we want to go, only some place that is equal, and if it's equal, why not stay here? There is nowhere else I would rather be."

"That is the statement of a happy, contented proprietor of a lovely tea room. And we have found it to be that. We hear Arthur in the background, your mina bird. Did he come with the shop?"

"My husband's search for night life took him to London one evening. He went out with a friend. He phoned me up at midnight and said, 'Will you bring 200 pounds down to London and meet me?' I said, 'Why? What's the matter?' He said, 'There's this bird . . . ,' then beep, beep, went the phone, and his money ran out. (Bird is another word for women in England.) I wasn't a very happy lady until I got to London and met Arthur. They were in a pub. Arthur was owned by two chaps in there who were in a bit of money trouble and wanted to get some cash and disappear, so we bought Arthur. If you listen carefully he has some wonderfully camp phrases. 'Allo, there.' 'You're *very* nice.' 'You're a big boy.' His laugh is wonderful. Once he laughs in the restaurant, everybody else starts laughing. And the more they laugh, the more he laughs. It's like having a ring full of laughing policemen."

"These are your paintings of the bridge from 1880?"

"Yes. Here are the maltings that stretch over where the present mooring is. That building was pulled down. The greenhouse is where we have our conservatory now. This is the same bridge from the other side. These are our upstairs bedroom windows. The paintings were done in payment to a previous owner by someone who was staying in the house. This lithograph was made in 1920. The maltings are gone, so we can date the approximate time they were pulled down."

"Your kitchen has a significant historical background."

"The kitchen is made from the altar at Snettisham Chapel. When the chapel was sold as a private dwelling, we bought all the internal fittings, the altar, and the stage that the altar sat on with lots of things like the little cupboards where the church books, Bibles, and prayerbooks lived. All the newel posts, in fact, became our stair rails going up to the top of the house. All the other wood was made into the kitchen. We paid a hundred pounds for all of it and have a very nice kitchen that should last for another 200 years."

"And your carpenter was?"

"The local undertaker. He was the best person, a very good carpenter, obviously, and also he is used to dealing with the old seasoned pine. You can't buy this kind of wood any longer. They only season oak now."

With the waning of our time, we slowly dismissed ourselves from the engaging conversation with the Kiltys with mutual good wishes expressed back and forth. We drove from The Bridge House Tea Rooms, past the luring apple tree to the GIs, and over the rebuilt bridge. We looked down on the lazy eddies of the Little Ouse and back toward the establishment graced by the river and its charming managers. We could understand the appeal felt by the American soldiers who reached out to the food offered.

## Loaf 6: Tea House Proprietor Dell Brower and The Essex Rose

When we visited Dedham, the area made famous by artist John Constable, we found an exquisite tea house, The Essex Rose, located in the central area of town. Mesmerized by the ambiance and quality, we sought an interview with the proprietor, Mr. Dell Brower, a charismatic host who roamed among the tables assuring himself that his guests were enjoying themselves and being cared for in a proper manner. When we returned, he resumed our interchange as amicably as though we had only had a five minute interruption. With the introduction and permissions noted on our tape, we continued.

"Will you tell us about your building?" I asked.

"The Essex Rose itself, the structure, is about circa 1500. During that period, Dedham was a thriving Flemish weaving center. And the large houses that you see here were where the master weavers used to live. These were the employers of the people, so for a long time they would have been the people who lived in these not using them for anything other than a private house. The people who worked for them would have lived in smaller cottages and done their work from there. The area has a varied history, and, as you can see, it is still very genuine. We try to keep the house as authentic as we can. This, of course, is enforced by the fact that it is a listed 'two scheduled building.' In England, this means you can't alter anything without permission. Not that you'd really want to, anyway. Colorwise, from the outside, we have to stick to the color that you see or there's a Suffolk tan, but you will see white, pink, or this tan color from the outside. The house has been used for various things. In the early '20s it was a general store. I don't have any photographs with me, but there was an exhibition of early photographs of Dedham and the area with one in particular of The Essex Rose with brushes and brooms and oil lamps outside. It was then used as a post office, then a private house again, and I would think that it's been used as an eating house for probably the last 50 years, no longer than that . . . and a tea house for about the last thirty. I, myself, with my wife and my daughter have been here for the last 15 years. As you know, by your experience of coming here, we are basically a tea house. With the change of all the fast food things, loads and loads of restaurants have appeared, but I am sure you will find on your travels that there are very, very few tea houses. The only thing we strayed away from on this is that we do what we term 'light lunches,' which are basically cold lunches with just a couple of things like soup, and pate, and jacket potatoes. Because that doesn't interfere with the prime factor of a tea house. And that's what we came here for—we feel that the tea house in all catering is about the nicest. On Sundays, like today, and bank holidays, in fact we will go through a thousand people in a day–that's coffee, lunch, and afternoon tea."

"We noticed on your business card that you manage this and direct it with your family. Could you tell us a bit about the family enterprise aspect?'

"Sure. It really must go back to our previous place when in fact we called it a tea garden. It was in the open air like you have lunch in the States, but we don't have weather for this. That came about 25 years ago when we bought a lovely, rural country cottage just outside Canterbury. My two children, my son and my daughter were then five and three respectively. And at that stage, I was not in the catering business at all. My wife had grown up in catering because her father is Italian and had restaurants all his life. We always thought that was an idyllic time in our life, probably because we found it when we could just about afford to buy it. The children were small, and the idea came, purely and simply, because it was one of the pretty little villages in Kent where no one was really supplying the need of the people that came. We were sitting ourselves having tea one afternoon, and the gate clicked, and about 40 people came walking up the garden path, you see, and said, 'Tea?' And we said, 'No. No. This is a private house.' But then my wife's mind started ticking and thinking, 'This is great, you know?' If you need to start something, you need a lot of permissions here. You don't just find a building and go ahead. We thought the first thing we'd do was put the idea before the parish council to turn the cottage into a tea garden. No problem at all, so we got planning permission for that.

We built on a huge cedar wood and glass extension. In those days, I did it all myself totally. We then paved two areas because British lawns don't stand up to our summers and people trampling across them. And that was really the very start of our experience. This is going to sound so small, and it was 25 years ago, but the very first day, we took in 18 pounds, the next day, we took 30, and the next day, we took 40 pounds, you know. And this was great. My wife was doing the baking, and we were both serving. We had nobody else then, because the children were both small. After about a month, we had the luxury of one dear lady who lived in the village doing the washing up, which we had done, and then we got a couple of waitresses, and then three waitresses, and it was tremendous success. You really have to be an extrovert like me, to like people, to need people to really feed on if you like. And that went on for about nine years. It was very successful. The one drawback came purely and simply from being conditional on the weather. It ran from Easter to the end of September. I was in the fashion business then, showing clothes, a house model of a big store in Canterbury, so my other work fit in well. My mother had moved down in Suffolk. I used to visit her. And, pure fairy story again really, she asked me to take her out to tea and bring her here. Which I did. As soon as I came to Dedham, I loved it. I'd never been to Dedham. Seventeen years ago, when I came here and saw this, I thought, 'That is fantastic.' I came back again with her. I talked to the owner, and said, 'I am going to be terribly presumptuous, but if you ever want to sell, would you contact me, and of course, the answer was, 'Good gracious, no,' as it would be, if somebody said it to me. But, then, two years later, her agent contacted me and said, 'I've been instructed to offer you The Essex Rose before we put it on the market.' That's how it started.

"Was it always named The Essex Rose? Or was that a name

you gave it?"

"It was named The Essex Rose and that was one of the things I bought with the rights of the property. It fits. Two of the combinations centering in the name were that it was where it is and has the association with the rose of Essex, but also, it used to have china with a Tudor rose on it. Unfortunately, we had to change that, because you can't get it anymore. As you see, we use a china called Indian Tree which is world-wide. It stemmed from the British Raj in India in all the tea houses there and this was the china that used to be used there. But the particular one that started with the place had to be replaced. We just couldn't find a supplier anymore for that china."

"I would like to ask you about the Dedham Mill adjacent, the origin, the date, and how long it was working."

"Sure. Dedham Mill was really brought to the world's light because it was one of the places that John Constable painted. It was always a working mill. The river in those days was navigable right the way up to it and beyond up to Sudbury with very narrow shallow draft barges. It was destroyed twice by fire in its history. I can't give you the exact date of the present mill. It could never replace the original. This has been closed and changed over to animal feedstuff, owned by the Clover family for many, many years. It stopped trading about three years ago. Purely demand, you know. And what is happening now, as you've probably seen, is a bit of a mess, because they sought planning permission to convert it into private accommodations, which in fact, for those of us already here, is a bit unfair, but we are here, and we keep a very sharp eye on whatever they do to Dedham. And I'm sure they didn't mean to do anything to spoil it, but the first plans were a little too large. They were overcrowded in here. We, in fact, settled really for 36 units that are going in there from studio flats up to very large ones, and I am pretty sure if we can forget what it looks like now, with its being demolished partly, and the work being done—if we can look at it in five years time when all the screening will be done, all the trees will be there, the land will be landscaped, the flowers will be there, and shrubs. I think it will fit in. I think it will be okay. The river, of course, is a lot more shallow. We only have row-boats and such on it. It is not navigable anymore at this point. The river is a trust which is a preservation society of various people, all sorts of people from all fields of life who spend an enormous amount of time, up to their thighs in mud, digging out and recovering old barges. They rebuild locks that have gone into decay, that kind of thing."

"And that is the church across the way that Constable made famous."

"Sure. And the thing your fellow Americans say to me is, 'It's huge.' Compared with the size of the village, it is huge. Very much so. And that is because in those days, Dedham was a thriving Flemish village. The master weavers put a lot of money into a church as large as that. But it is a very prosperous church, a very well looked after church, certainly not just from the parishioners of Dedham. People from Colchester come . . . I am sure you can hear the noise on the interview tape now, because we been invaded by a coach, but that's what our business is, so that's good for me."

"It seems to me that the British proprietors do not seem so pressed as Americans do. If something is successful in one place you don't feel the need to make it a chain and put it in every little town."

"Sure. And in this, I would agree with you totally. It's not really a case of that. It's the case that here, we have a management question. I don't know whether it's the same in the States—I mean, I found very successful restaurants in chains being run by managers. But here, who do we split up? If we open another business which has been in our minds in all the other villages around for ages, sure, we could do that, but who runs it? We feel that the Brower family is The Essex Rose. The people come because it's The Essex Rose, but they come because we are here. That presents problems. It means that the three of us never go away together anymore. We have to split holidays and things like that. One of the Browers is here with our staff. The public knows one of us is always here. Yes, the temptation has been with me all the time to open one, then another one, and another one. When I put this to the bank, they said, 'Sure, great idea, but where will we find a cardboard Dell Brower to put in another shop?' That's exactly the problem we feel in England. In the States, when I was there, I was losing incidentally, because the friends I made were tempting me enormously to open a Tea House in West Palm Beach, of all places, but just one. Open that as the picture, and then franchise the whole thing after a year, which I'm sure would work in the States. I'm not sure we are ready for franchising in our business. The McDonald's and pizza parlors work in England, but I'm not sure tea houses like ours would work that way. I rather think not."

"A few minutes ago when you mentioned the crowd coming in reminded me of a question we had. We imagined your business would be two-fold, that from people who would be here year-round, and a pick-up and increase in business when you would have the tourist season."

"That is exactly right. This one bus we didn't know about, but you can see we coped with it perfectly. There must have been 60 people arrive amongst the people who were already here who are the everyday patrons. From now on, we are expecting the tourist people will come. From November to April, it's mostly local people, but local as far as 40 miles away. They'll come down on Sunday afternoon to tea. We will do

fivefold business from June 1 to the end of September. It never presents
a problem because we now think we are pros. I don't mind what anybody does in anything, but I love pros who are pros at everything they
do. I don't like amateurs, really, those people who play at business.
Amateurs tend to spoil business for the people who run good businesses. We never close. We do close three days: Christmas Day,
Boxing Day, and the day after. We are open every day except those
three. People come time and time again. They know we are here. The
problem with people coming is no problem. The problem is people not
coming. I never understand anybody who says, 'Oh, my goodness, it's
terrible to cope with.' It is far harder when you don't do business."

"We were interested also in your menu. Do you serve the same
kinds of things for tea? Will you vary it in the course of a year? Or
will you stick with the traditional dishes? We were also interested in
the term 'cream tea.' What is the significance of that? What is the
difference between 'set tea' and 'cream tea?'

"Sure. We do. From about November 1, we bring in tea cakes,
toasted tea cakes, toasted scones, the same scones you had yesterday.
We toast those. We will toast anything like that. That alters the afternoon tea. The term, 'cream tea,' of course, this we must really give back
to the people who originated it. It was in Devonshire. Their milk is
totally different from any other part, and they have this lovely great
clotted cream. In all the farmhouses, the farm workers wives would
make their scones and set this cream in great big pans on a very, very
slow heat. All the cream is skimmed off to make clotted cream which
has spread worldwide to have with scones and strawberry jam. Always
with strawberry jam. Fresh cream and strawberry jam. So that is the
cream tea part. The tray tea as you saw is either one of two things. We
have fresh cream gateaux, which are totally fresh cream, black forest,
lemon torte, which is originally an Austrian recipe, and that is a lemon

mousse center on a biscuit base covered in fresh cream. And then we have strawberry gateaux which is layers of sponge with crushed strawberries in between again covered with fresh cream and decorated with strawberries. Our own cake tray looks more like an ordinary cake tray that is a variety of plain sponges—Victoria sponges—chocolate sponges, coffee sponges—decorated with butter cream rather than fresh cream. And then we offer the variety of those on the tray with fresh cream eclairs and all of our biscuit range, chocolate, Florentines, flapjacks which is what we call a crunch biscuit, or short bread, which is world-wide. So they are really the three teas that we do.

"Is the set tea the same as the cream tea in different areas?"

"The set tea really is something they want you to have as a set. It can consist certainly of scones, cream, and jam and your tea, and a little sandwich. Specifically, if we go downwards from the Ritz, it will be a selection of little sandwiches, cucumber, smoked salmon, tiny little triangles, and then you will have scones, cream, and jam, and then some pastries, and your tea. Now, that is the Ritz set tea. But you are quite right that other areas will do other things for their tea. High tea is more in the north, and that would be in that area mostly fish and chips tea, or salad, something like this, bread and butter, but they would be something like five o'clock in the afternoon for people who want that. Again, we do that if someone wants a salad tea on booked parties. We really can't do that as individuals, although we would treat it as the person came because of the number of people around. Like this afternoon, we are seating 90 in the three rooms, and this afternoon, unless I am totally wrong, from 4:30 until we close, there will be all those tables full and people waiting out the door for the tables, as well. So you have to really do on basis what people come for—the three teas that we do.

"We are grateful to you, Mr. Brower, for your time this morning and that of your lovely family. We have appreciated your being willing to talk to us."

"You are very welcome, ma'am. If I may put in, and you can do this, it's a little reward because you know. . . I mean this in the nicest way. None of us when we go to different countries always are accepted in the right way. I mean, you come over and wave the American flag exactly the right way. Other tourists come over and set their backs up with people. When I went down to the States two years ago for the Rider Cup to West Palm Beach, I received wonderful hospitality. I mean, my comments to people always since I have come back is, 'Go, and stay with the people. That's when you know them. That's when you meet them. Stay in their homes, and you have a job then, to pay the bill.' And so you are very welcome for the interview and I hope that your book will be a great success. Please. When you publish it, send me one, at least."

"When we do, you can count on it. Thank you again."

We retraced our way from Dedham, satisfied with the fare and filled with the friendship of another marvelous host of a tea shop in East Anglia.

Loaves and hyacinths.

Loaves and hyacinths.

# Works Consulted

Anderson, Kenneth. *Coffees and Teas: How to Select, Brew, and Appreciate the Finest Coffees and Teas*. New York: Perigree, 1982.

Brabbs, Derry. *English Country Churches*. New York: Viking, 1985.

Forman, Joan. *Haunted East Anglia*. Norwich: Jarrold and Sons, Ltd., 1985.

Franklin, Aubrey. *Teatime by the Tea Ambassador*. New York: Frederick Fell Publishers, 1981.

Hesse, Eelco. *Tea: The Eyelids of Bodhidharma*. Stable Court: Prism Press, 1982.

Hogg, Garry, and John Tomes. *Exploring Britain*. London: A&C Black, 1985.

Isles, Joanna. *A Proper Tea*. New York: St. Martin's, 1989.

Israel, Andrea, and Pamela Mitchell. *Taking Tea: The Essential Guide to Brewing, Serving, and Entertaining with Teas from Around the World*. New York: Weidenfeld and Nicolson, 1987.

Jackson, Stanley. *The Savoy: The Romance of a Great Hotel*. London: Frederick Muller, Ltd., 1984.

Kakuzo, Okakura. *The Book of Tea*. 1906. Rutland, Vermont: Charles E. Tuttle, 1970.

Laughlin, Clara E. *So You're Going to England*. Boston: Houghton, 1928.

Maps. *East Anglia Guide*. Hadleigh, Suffolk: East Anglia Tourist Board, 1986.

McCurdy, Sylvia. *Sylvia: A Victorian Childhood*. Lavenham: Eastland Press, 1972.

McKenney, Ruth, and Richard Bransten. *Here's England*. New York: Harper, 1971.

Mehling, Franz N., ed. *Great Britain and Ireland: A Phaidon Cultural Guide*. Englewood Cliffs, N.J.: Prentice-Hall, 1985.

Simpson, Helen. *The London Ritz Book of Afternoon Tea: The Art and Pleasures of Taking Tea*. London: Ebury Press, 1986.

Simpson, Norman T. *Country Inns and Back Roads*. Cambridge: Harper, 1985.

Smedley, Norman. *Life and Tradition in Suffolk and North-east Essex*. London: Dent, 1976.

Tenison, Marika Hanbury. *Book of Afternoon Tea*. Devon: David and Charles Publishers, 1980.

Walkling, Gillian. *Tea Caddies: An Illustrated History*. London: The Victoria and Albert Museum, 1985.

Ward, Zoe. *Curtsy to the Lady*. Lavenham: Terence Dalton Limited, 1985.

West, H. Mills. *Colourful Characters from East Anglia*. Great Yarmouth: Galliard, 1986.

Whipple, Andy, and Rob Anderson. *The English Pub*. New York: Viking, 1985.